Relics From the Wreck of a Former World, or, Splinters Gathered on the Shores of a Turbulent Planet

RELICS FROM THE WRECK

OF

A FORMER WORLD;

OR

SPLINTERS GATHERED ON THE SHORES

OF

A TURBULENT PLANET,

&c.; &c.; &c.

ILLUSTRATED WITH ENGRAVINGS.

NEW-YORK:
W. H. GRAHAM, TRIBUNE BUILDINGS;
H. LONG AND BROTHER, 32 ANN STREET;
BURGESS, STRINGER & CO. 222 BROADWAY.

RELICS

FROM THE WRECK OF A FORMER WORLD;

OR,

SPLINTERS GATHERED ON THE SHORES

OF

A TURBULENT PLANET.

PROVING,

TO A DEMONSTRATION, THE VAST ANTIQUITY OF THE EARTH; AND, THE
EXISTENCE OF ANIMAL LIFE—OF THE MOST FANTASTIC SHAPES,
AND THE MOST ELEGANT COLORS: RIVALING THOSE
OF THE RAINBOW,—MILLIONS OF YEARS BE-
FORE THE APPEARANCE OF MAN.

WITH AN APPENDIX

ON THE SCENERY IN A PATCH OF INFINITE SPACE. TO WHICH IS ADDED,
ACCOUNTS OF THE MOST WONDERFUL BODIES, AND SUBSTANCES,
THAT HAVE FALLEN FROM HEAVEN, IN ALL AGES OF
THE WORLD: WITH AN ANALYSIS
OF EACH.

ILLUSTRATED WITH ENGRAVINGS.

" It will not do for Christians to deny the conclusion, on the ground that the Mosaic
narrative teaches that the Earth is only about *six thousand years old.* Thus is attribut
ing to Moses a sentiment which his language does not justify."—*W. Lindsay Alexander*
D D, F S A S

NEW YORK:

W. H. GRAHAM, TRIBUNE BUILDINGS, II LONG &
BROTHER, 32 ANN-STREET, AND BURGESS,
STRINGER & CO, 222 BROADWAY.

1847.

PREFACE.

Eternal truth! how wondrous is thy power,
How vain the human mind to fully trace
All the deep mysteries that hover o'er
The hidden depths of thy profound embrace.

THE present work is intended to furnish a general
view of the leading appearances of Physical Nature—the
economy of the heavens and the earth: deduced from
Milner's "Gallery of Nature," Mantell's "Medals of
Creation," and other authentic sources.

Geology and Astronomy are, in truth, sciences
whose discoveries have realized the wildest imaginings
of the poet, and whose *realities* infinitely surpass, in
grandeur and sublimity, the most imposing fictions of
romance.

RELICS

FROM THE WRECK OF A FORMER WORLD.

CHAPTER I.

"The very ground on which we tread, and the mountains which surround us, may be regarded as vast tumuli, in which the organic remains of a former world are enshrined."—*Parkinson's Org Rem , Vol. I.*

ACCUSTOMED to consider the whole of nature as having sprung out of nothing at the Divine command in the course of a few days—and *erroneously* deeming this belief as essentially connected with the fundamental articles of Christian faith—it is little wonder when Hutton announced to the world that the earth offered no trace of a commencement, nor any prospect of an end, that he was assailed as an infidel. But time effects changes in the moral as well as the physical world, and such a belief is *now* considered no way obnoxious to a *true* interpretation of the *sacred* text.

Some of our divines are among the most celebrated geologists, and the vast antiquity of the earth *has* become as fully accredited as if it had formed a distinct subject of revelation. A few cavillers are still to be found, but not among the enlightened portion of the Christian community. It is only from those who, assuming *their* preconceptions to be true, and *their* interpretations of Scripture right, that we find any opposition to the stubborn evidence of fact.

"The hope of truth grows stronger day by day;
I hear the soul of Man around me waking,
Like a great sea its frozen fetters breaking,
And flinging up to heaven its sunlit spray,
Tossing huge continents in scornful play,
And crushing them with din of grinding thunder
That makes old emptiness stare in wonder."

Disputation is an irksome and thankless employment, and scarcely answers the purpose of conviction, because the mind naturally sets up its own *old* defences whenever its *prejudices* are attacked. "Men do not willingly," says the Rev. Thomas Milner, "abandon notions that have grown with their growth, and strengthened with their strength, and struck their roots deep and fast into their 'heart of hearts.' Besides being mortifying to intellectual vanity to admit an error, they disrelish the mental disturbance occasioned by the breaking up of old associations of ideas, and the toil which a correct conception of truth may require. Much of the suspicion with which the scientific have been visited, may be referred to prejudices in favor of early imbibed opinions, to which the demonstrations of science have been opposed—prejudices which are known in the pages of Lord Bacon as *idola specus*, the individual mind being the den to which that sagacious observer of human nature alludes, and repugnant as it is to the owner and guardian of the mental cavern to have its chambers of imagery searched, and the occupant of any niche ejected, men have been compelled repeatedly to submit to the process, however they may have resisted the attempt. A country schoolmaster may still discourse of the four elements—fire, air, earth, and water; and his boys may look up to him as a prodigy of erudition; but chemical analysis teaches us to smile at the enumeration, though old as the days of the Greek philosophers. So the antiquated notion of the earth being an extended plane, like a table,—as motionless as that household instrument, the sun coming to take his daily peep at it, like a careful watchman on his rounds,—has vanished from the face of civilized society, though supported by the impression of the senses, once deemed essential to religious faith, and defended by ecclesiastical law. It becomes us therefore, when the decisions of science are contrary to our familiar ideas, to inquire into the soundness of both, and willingly to surrender our preconceived opinions to the force of truth, and not to any *prejudice* against *knowledge.*"

The vast antiquity of our globe is now as fully demonstrated as its *rotundity :* and the lapse of ages which *must* have occurred in the completion of a geological epoch, *as evident as the distances of the heavenly spheres :* indeed more so—because the one can be proven to any person in the *slightest* degree conversant with the structure of the earth, by deductions *most* rational and satisfactory, and by evidence the *most* complete; whereas in Astronomy the person who cannot apply the telescopic tube, has in a great measure to rest satisfied with the testimony of the astronomer, and the collateral evidence of the mathematician. That our globe was the seat of animal and vegetable life through a countless series of ages, before its occupation by the human species—that successive races flourished, decayed and altogether vanished, long anterior to the appearance of man upon the stage of life—is a conclusion of which irrefragable evidence is afforded in the myriad forms of once animated existence, whose remains have been disinterred from their graves in the lias, gypsum-quarries, and chalk, and which enter almost exclusively into the composition of vast masses of mountain limestone.

"The earth is in truth a charnel house, full of bones, sinews, shells, leaves, and prostrate trunks, and with consummate skill the botanist and comparative anatomist have traced the animal and vegetable forms indicated by the fragments gathered from the wreck of life. Ancient conditions of our planet have thus been restored, when stately

ferns and graceful palms threw their shadows upon its surface, and herbivorous and carnivorous quadrupeds roamed
in its forests ; when animate objects of uncouth shape
swarmed in its rivers, and sported on its plains ; all, however, swept away antecedent to the human creation, and
whose skeletons, after being washed in the ocean, were
laid up in the solid masonry of the globe's present super-
structure. The current of popular opinion has run violently against statements of this kind ; *for no sentiment
has stronger hold of the common mind, than that all the
alarming phenomena of nature, with the existence of
death in the animal kingdom, are the penal consequences
of human transgression.* Poetry has helped to extend
and perpetuate this idea, which observation contradicts, and
which a rational exegesis of the Scripture testimony has
shown to be unsupported by the record from which it was
primarily derived.

> ' Thus began
> Outrage from lifeless things ; but Discord first
> Daughter of Sin, among the irrational,
> Death introduced, through fierce antipathy ,
> Beast now with beast 'gan war, and fowl with fowl,
> And fish with fish ; to graze the herb all leaving,
> Devour'd each other ; nor stood much in awe
> Of man, but fled him ; or with countenance grim
> Glared on him passing.'

"The opening verse of the Scriptures announces the fact
of a dependant universe being created by the Almighty, *but
assigns no date to the mighty operation.* Geology demands nothing beyond what this indefinite enunciation of
the Creator's work as to time supplies ; and theology, in the
passage, requires only an acknowledgment of the will, power,
and wisdom of the one God, in originating and super-
intending the terrestrial constitution. At a precise point
of time, the earth, in its primordial elements, as we are left

quite at liberty to conceive, was called into being, *but the question is completely undetermined when that time was.* An interval as long as the imagination can entertain may be placed between the *first* operation of Divine power, and the *subsequent* arrangement of the globe for the habitation of man. The record allows room enough for all those wonderful changes and transformations to transpire, the indubitable memorials of which are discovered in the deep and dark places of the earth, which, after ages of entombment, have been commanded to show themselves; but yet, as if to prevent man from becoming proud amid the triumphs of his genius, he is checked at once in the endeavor to measure the interval, the vastness of which he can discern, which will ever remain to us in the present state, invested with the obscurity that marks the number of the ocean's sands. There has been, however, no little flippancy and contraction of mind evinced by many who have carped at the demands of geological time, for time is long or short according to the particular standard we employ in its measurement."—*Milner.*

At the first step we take in geological inquiry, says the Rev. Dr. Buckland, we are struck with the immense period of time which the phenomena presented to our view *must* have required for their production, and the incessant changes which appear to have been going on in the natural world; but we must remember that time and change are great, only in reference to the *faculties* of the being who notes them. The insect of an hour contrasting its own ephemeral existence with the flowers on which it rests, would attribute an unchanging durability to the most evanescent of vegetable forms, while the flowers, the trees, and the forest would ascribe an endless duration to the soil on which they grow; and thus, uninstructed man comparing his own brief earthly existence with the solid frame-work of the world he inhabits, deems the hills and mountains around him coeval

with the globo itself. But with the enlargement and culti-
vation of his mental powers, he takes a moro just, compre-
hensive, and enlightened view of the wonderful scheme of
creation, and while in his ignorance he imagined that the
duration of the globe was to be measured by his own brief
span, and arrogantly deemed himself alone the object of the
Almighty's care, and that all things were created for his
pleasure and necessities, he now feels his dependence, enter-
tains more correct ideas of the mercy, wisdom, and goodness of his Creator; and while exercising his high privilege
of being alone capable of contemplating and understanding
the wonders of the natural world, he learns the most important of all lessons—to doubt the evidence of his own
senses until confirmed by patient and cautious investiga-
tions.

" Where is the dust that has not been alive ?"

The remains of organic existence, found in the median
and other tertiaries, conduct us from the colossal and imposing to the minute and microscopic ; for beds occur entirely
composed of the fossil relics of animalculites— those infinitesimal forms now present in our lakes, rivers, and
streams, invisible to the unassisted sight, whose perfect organization places them among the wonders of the creation.
They were formerly supposed to be little more than mere
particles of matter endowed with vitality; but Ehrenberg
has discovered in them an apparatus of muscles, intestines,
teeth, different kinds of glands, eyes, nerves, and organs of
reproduction.   Yet some of the smallest are not more than
the 24,000th of an inch in diameter, the thickness of the
skin of their stomachs not more than the 50,000,000th part
of an inch, a single drop of water having been estimated
sometimes actually to contain 500,000,000 individuals.
Not less astonishing is their power of multiplication, an individual of one species increasing in ten days to 1,000,000

on the eleventh day to 4,000,000, and on the twelfth day to
16,000,000; while, of another kind, Ehrenberg states that one
individual is capable of becoming, in four days, 170,000,-
000,000! To this distinguished naturalist we are indebted
for the developement of the fact that ages ago our world
was rife with these minute organisms, belonging to a great
number of species, whose mineralised skeletons actually constitute nearly the whole mass of some tertiary soils and rocks
several feet in thickness, and extending over areas of many
acres. Such is the *Polirschiefer*, or polishing slate of Bilin
in Bohemia, which occupies a surface of great extent, probably the site of an ancient lake, and forms slaty strata of
fourteen feet in thickness, almost wholly composed of the
silicified shields of animalcules. The size of a single one,
forming the polishing slate, " amounts upon an average, and
in the greatest part, to $\frac{1}{288}$ of a line, which equals $\frac{1}{4}$ of
the thickness of a human hair, reckoning its average
size at $\frac{1}{72}$ of a line. The globule of the human blood
considered at $\frac{1}{300}$ is not much smaller. The blood glo-
bules of a frog are twice as large as one of these animalcules. As the Polirschiefer of Bilin is slaty, but
without cavities, these animalcules lie closely compressed.
In round numbers, about 23 millions would make up a cubic
line, and would in fact be contained in it. There are 1728
cubic lines in a cubic inch; and therefore a cubic inch
would contain, on an average, about 41,000 millions of
these animals. On weighing a cubic inch of this mass,
I found it to be about 220 grains. Of the 41,000 millions
of animals 187 millions go to a grain; or the siliceous
shield of each animalcule weighs about $\frac{1}{187}$ millionth part of
a grain." Such is the statement of Ehrenberg, which naturally suggests to the reflection of the French philosopher,
that if the Almighty is great in great things, he is still
more so in those which are minute; and furnishes additional
data for the well-known moral argument of the theologian

derived from a comparison of the telescope and microscope :—
"The one led me to see a system in every star; the other
leads me to see a world in every atom. The one taught me
that this mighty globe, with the whole burden of its people
and of its countries, is but a grain of sand on the high field
of immensity.* The other teaches me, that every grain of
sand may harbor within it the tribes and the families of a
busy population. The one told me of the insignificance
of the world I tread upon. The other redeems it from all
insignificance; for it tells me that

"In the leaves of every forest, in the flowers of every garden, in the
waters of every rivulet, there are worlds teeming with life, and numberless as are the glories of the firmament."—*Rev Dr Chalmers.*

Nothing more perfectly demonstrates the power of Nature
to effect her vast designs through apparently feeble and in-
sufficient agents, than the coral formation. It requires,
indeed, ocular proof of the labors of the madrepores, to
credit what stupendous submarine reefs and islands, many
miles in compass, are indebted for at least a great part of
their structure to the secretory economy of these minute
artificers.

The coral insects are abundant in the Mediterranean,
where corallines of beautiful forms and colors are produced;
but it is in the Pacific Ocean and its branches that these

---

* Sir John Herschel, in an "Essay on the Power of the Telescope to
penetrate into space," a quality distinct from the magnifying power, in-
forms us that there are stars so infinitely remote as to be situated at the
distance of *twelve millions of millions of millions of miles* from our earth,
so that light, which travels with a velocity of twelve millions of miles
in a minute, would require *two millions of years* for its transit from those
distant orbs to our own; while the astronomer who should record the aspect or mutations of such a star, would be relating, not its history at the
present day, *but that which took place two millions of years gone by* And
when we reflect that if it were possible for us to attain to those distant
spheres, we should look, not on the limits, the blank wall of Creation,
but only into *fresh* fields of Creation, Power, and Wisdom, we feel that
our earth and all that it inherits is a mere speck in space, an atom amid
the vast Universe —(See Appendix.)

tiny workmen are effecting those mighty changes, which far exceed the most remarkable labors of man.

> "Millions of millions thus from age to age,
> With simplest skill, and toil unweariable,
> No moment and no movement unimproved,
> Laid line on line, on terrace terrace spread,
> To swell the heightening, brightening gradual mound,
> By marvellous structure climbing towards the day.
> Each wrought alone, yet altogether wrought,
> Unconscious, not unworthy, instruments,
> By which a hand invisible was rearing
> A new creation in the secret deep
> Omnipotence wrought in them, with them, by them;
> Hence what Omnipotence alone could do
> Worms did. I saw the living pile ascend,
> The mausoleum of its architects,
> Still dying upwards as their labors closed:
> Slime the material, but the slime was turn'd
> To adamant, by their petrific touch;
> Frail were their frames, ephemeral their lives,
> Their masonry imperishable. All
> Life's needful functions, food, exertion, rest,
> By nice economy of Providence
> Were overruled to carry on the process
> Which out of water brought forth solid rock.
> Atom by atom thus the burthen grew,
> Even like an infant in the womb, till Time
> Deliver'd ocean of that monstrous birth—
> A coral island stretching east and west."

That those infinitesimal forms of existence, whose presence in our lakes, rivers, and streams, can only be made manifest by the aid of the microscope, should be detected in a fossil state, and that their aggregated skeletons should be found to constitute the chains of hills, and the subsoil of extensive districts, and that the most stupendous monuments erected by man, should be composed of rocks resulting from the mineralized remains of animalcules, invisible to the unassisted eye, are among the most marvellous of wonders.*

---

* If we apply our vision to the microscope, we behold in every leaf and blade of grass, and every drop of water in which these substances have

Every walk we take offers subjects for profound consideration—every pebble that attracts our notice, matter for serious reflection; and contemplating the innumerable proofs afforded us of the incessant dissolution and renovation which are taking place around us, we feel the force and beauty of the exclamation of the poet,

> " My heart is awed within me, when I think
> Of the great miracle which still goes on
> In silence round me — the perpetual work
> Of Thy creation, finished, yet renewed
> For ever !"

---

become decomposed, a world of life and being, unknown, unseen by the feeble human eye. We have *only to cut a little hay into small pieces with a pair of scissors, put the pieces into a saucer full of water, and let them stand for a week, when a film will appear on the surface, which we have but to take off with a spoon, put it under the microscope, and we have then before us in the mere drop of water a world of animated beings of high order of organization, possessing heads, eyes, with systems nervous, circulatory, respiratory, and digestive, yet the creatures themselves so infinitely minute as to be perfectly invisible to the most acute and perfect sight.* The animalculæ form, in fact, one of the most important realms in the vast empire of Nature, and so vast are their numbers, their species and the diversified phenomena of their existence, that, as with the vast and unnumbered orbs above us, the mind is lost in the immensity of the contemplation ; we find that the infinitely minute, like the infinitely magnificent, transcends our powers of observation, and we are left to admire, to wonder, and adore

CHAPTER II.*

——" Let the moon
Shine on thee in thy solitary walk;
And let the misty mountain winds be free
To blow against thee; and in after years,
When these wild ecstasies shall be matured
Into a sober pleasure — when thy mind
Shall be a mansion for all lovely forms,
Thy memory be a dwelling place
For all sweet sounds and harmonies, oh! then
If solitude, or fear, or pain, or grief
Should be thy portion, with what healing thoughts
Of tender joy wilt thou remember me
And these my benedictions!" WORDSWORTH

IN walking over the surface of a country, we witness its undulations, its mountains, and its rivers, and are apt to conclude that hill and valley, river and lake, may have existed in nearly the same condition since time began its ceaseless course. But when we come to examine the structure of the mountain, the causes of undulation, the alterations which have taken place in the water courses, nay, even in the general configuration of the globe itself, or of any particular region of it, we naturally exclaim, "the hills themselves are the daughters of time, the waves of the present ocean played in past ages on other shores, and the rivers which supply it are derived from surfaces, which in ancient days were below the level of the deep—all that is now land, is but the debris† of continents and islands now unknown; *the wreck of a former world*—the spoils and the sport of time."

Effects have been produced, which, if attributed to the

---

* See chapter v., p. 45.   † The waste of other rocks.

ordinary agencies of Nature, require the imagination to
stretch its visual glance through the vista of a past eter-
nity, or at least through a lapse of ages, as inconceivable in
duration, as the distances of the spheres are in the field of
space.

"Were we to assert," says the Rev. Dr. Buckland, "that
the present continents of Europe, Asia, Africa, and America,
*were once wholly immersed under the waters of the ocean,
and that after rising at different spots in low newborn
islands,** they gradually acquired their present configuration ; nay, that the whole materials of which both the
present continents and their islands are composed, have
resulted from the denudation of continents and islands
which have been worn away, or finally sunk under the all-*

---

* One circumstance may well surprise us, and that is, to find in the
Bible mountains distinguished in *two* classes, very nearly in the manner as
they are distinguished by science into *primitive* and *secondary* Thus in
the 104th Psalm, a composition of incomparable poetical beauty, the prophet gives us an idea of the formation of the earth ; *he represents it to us
as still covered with the waters of the deep as with a garment The
waters stood above all the mountains, but many of these eminences became
elevated, and rose above their level; the waters then retired and fled
New mountains then appeared, and valleys, and plains, the lowest parts of
the globe were formed at their feet* Two principal epochs, then, must
have been in the mind of the prophet, from the time of the rising up of
the heights which appear on all parts of the globe ; these two epochs cor-
respond to the formation of primitive and secondary mountains

Reference is even made to the force by which they have been elevated .
it is represented as proportionate to the elevation to which their eminences have been raised, being most powerful when employed in elevating
the mountains properly so called, and weaker when its efforts were limit-
ed to the raising of the hills above the valleys In its figurative style, it
compares the elevation of the former to the skipping of rams, and that
of the latter to the leaping of lambs. Newton esteemed the Bible "the
most authentic of all histories;" Hale said, "none was like unto it for
excellent wisdom, learning, and use," Boyle considered it "a matchless
volume, impossible to be too much studied or too highly esteemed ;" and
Locke pronounced it as "consisting of Truth without any mixture of Error
for its matter."

encroaching · influence of · the waves, we would not be credited by many—the assertion would seem that of one whose avocation was the excitement of astonishment, and who if he could make his reader wonder, had attained the acme of his ambition. Yet such, nevertheless, is the conclusion, to which all who study the structure of the earth, divested of prejudice and preconception, are necessarily led."

If we look with wonder upon the great remains of human works, says Sir H. Davy, such as the columns of Palmyra, broken in the midst of the desert; the temples of Pæstum, beautiful in the decay of twenty centuries; or the mutilated fragments of Greek sculpture in the Acropolis of Athens, or in our own museums, as proofs of the genius of artists, and power and riches of nations now passed away; with how much deeper feeling of admiration must we consider those grand monuments of nature which mark the revolutions of the Globe; continents broken into islands; one land produced, another destroyed; the bottom of the ocean become a fertile soil; whole races of animals extinct, and the bones and exuviæ of one class covered with the remains of another; and upon the graves of past generations—the marble or rocky tombs, as it were, of a former animated world—new generations rising, and order and harmony established, and a system of life and beauty produced out of chaos and death; proving the infinite power, wisdom, and goodness of the GREAT CAUSE of all things!

From the numerous foreign writers, who at a very early period began to entertain correct notions of the structure of our planet, and of the nature of the revolutions which it had undergone, we are induced to select the following highly philosophical and beautiful illustration of the physical mutations to which the surface of the earth is perpetually exposed. It is from an Arabic manuscript written in the thirteenth century. The narrative is supposed to be given by Rhidhz, an allegorical personage.

"I passed one day by a very ancient and populous city and I asked one of its inhabitants how long it had been founded? 'It is, indeed, a mighty city,' replied he; 'we know not how long it has existed, and our ancestors were on this subject as ignorant as ourselves.' Some centuries afterwards, as I passed by the same place, I could not perceive the slightest vestige of the city. I demanded of a peasant, who was gathering herbs upon its former site, how long it had been destroyed?' 'In sooth, a strange question,' replied he, 'the ground here has never been different from what you now behold it.' 'Was there not,' said I, 'of old a splendid city here?' 'Never,' answered he, 'so far as we know, and never did our fathers speak to us of any such.'

"On my return there again, after the lapse of other centuries, I found the sea in the same place, and on its shores were a party of fishermen, of whom I inquired how long the land had been covered by the waters? 'Is this a question', said they, 'for a man like you? This spot has always been what it is now.'

"I again returned ages afterwards, and the sea had disappeared. I inquired of a man who stood alone upon the ground, how long the change had taken place, and he gave me the same answer that I had received before.

"Lastly, on coming back again after an equal lapse of time, I found there a flourishing city, more populous and more rich in buildings than the city I had seen the first time; and when I would have fain informed myself regarding its origin, the inhabitants answered me, 'its rise is lost in remote antiquity—we are ignorant how long it has existed, and our fathers were on this subject no wiser than ourselves.' "

We may smile at the ignorance of the inhabitants of the fabled cities, but are we in a condition to give a more satisfactory reply should it be inquired of us, 'What are the physical changes which the country you inhabit has undergone?—and yet cautious observation, and patient and unprejudiced investigation, are alone necessary to enable us to answer the interrogation.

Dismissing from his mind all preconceived opinions, the student must be prepared to discover that the earth's surface has been, and still is, subject to perpetual mutation, —that the sea and land are continually changing place,— that what is now dry land was once the bottom of the deep, and that the bed of the present ocean will, in its turn, be elevated above the water and become dry land,—that all the solid materials of the globe have been in a softened, fluid, or gaseous state,—and that the remains of countless myriads of animals and plants are not only entombed in the rocks and mountains, but that every grain of sand, and every particle of dust wafted by the wind, may teem with the relics of beings that lived and died in periods long antecedent to the creation of the human race. Astounding as are these propositions, they rest upon evidence so clear and incontrovertible, that they cannot fail to be admitted by every intelligent and unprejudiced reader, who will bestow but a moderate share of attention to the phenomena, of which it is the purport of this work to offer a familiar exposition.

Scott, in his "Marmion," refers to a legend once prevalent in the neighborhood of Whitby, that the ammonite shells, which are common in that vicinity, had formerly been snakes, which the foundress of the abbey, St. Hilda, succeeded in decapitating by her prayers, and then converting into stone:—

> " And how the nuns of Whitby told,
> How of countless snakes, each one
> Was changed into a coil of stone—
> When holy Hilda pray'd.
> Themselves within their sacred bound
> Their stony folds had often found."

We shall now proceed to lay before the reader some of the data connected with the stratification of the earth, which

lead to the conclusion of a vast antiquity, and of the
physical revolutions it has undergone since it has become
a planet. Our limits forbid us from entering into detail on
all the multifarious forms which geology has disclosed to
our observation, nor, were we doing so, could it prove interesting to any of our readers, except such as have made
comparative anatomy more or less their study, nor will our
limits allow of more than a general notice of the most remarkable of those forms which peopled our planet *prior* to
the existence of our own species.

"Every rock in the desert, every boulder on the plain, every pebble by
the brook-side, every grain of sand on the sea-shore, is replete with lessons of wisdom to the mind that is fitted to receive and comprehend their
sublime import."

The rocks of which the crust of the earth is chiefly composed, occur in beds or layers, on examining them we find
every evidence of their having resulted from matter carried
by rivers into lakes, estuaries, or seas This is demonstra-
ble from some of them being composed of fragments of
other rocks worn and rounded by the action of water, so as not
to be distinguished from the gravel strewed upon the shore,
or which we meet with in the path of a mountain stream,
except in its having been consolidated into a stony mass—
such rocks are called *conglomerates.* The red sandstone
formations of Arran, and the coasts of Argyle and Ayrshire,
Scotland, consist of immense beds of such rocks, alternat-
ing with layers of red clay, and red sandstone. This formation itself is many thousand feet thick ; we never find in
it any fragments of the coal, or of any newer formation ;
on the contrary, the conglomerates consist solely of pieces
of quartz, slate, red sandstone, and other rocks of more
ancient date. In the same formation, which stretches from
Argyle through Stirlingshire and Forfarshire, to the eastern
coast, remains of fishes in a very perfect state of preservation,
have been found. In both the conglomerates then, and in the

fishes we have evidence of this formation having been produced, *not instantaneously*, but through a long succession of ages. Each bed of pebbles, if the ancient agencies of nature were any way analogous to the present, must have been the work of many years. That these agencies *were not more violent*, or at least that there were long intervals of repose, *is attested by the beds of fine grained sandstone, and consolidated mud, with which the conglomerates alternate.* The largest of our existing rivers, in rainy seasons, carry great quantities of gravel, sand and mud, into their estuaries or the sea; but great as the amount of debris is, the production of a quantity of matter, any way equivalent to the old red sandstones of England and Scotland, could not take place except in the lapse of innumerable ages. The mud carried down by the Nile, and deposited, amounts only to *a quarter of an inch thick annually.* The old red sandstone formation is estimated at from three to four thousand yards in thickness. Allowing *a quarter of an inch* as the average annual aggregation of matter, this formation alone could not have been deposited in less than 432,000 years.

If we contemplate for a moment the agencies that must have been engaged in wearing down the surfaces of the ancient rocks, and in transporting them over the vast areas they now occupy, the time here stated will not seem any way exaggerated, but far too little for the amount of the effects produced. We have mentioned the old red sandstone formation as an instance, from which something like an idea may be formed of the time requisite for the production of a certain class of rocks. The same, or even still more decisive proofs of the lapse and change of time are afforded by the other formations.

To disintegrate to any considerable extent a solid rock — to transfer the material by a river-current to any oceanic site to deposit it, and consolidate the deposition, are excessively slow operations, requiring the lapse of centuries to accomplish the formation of a thin stratum. We are certain, therefore, that the building up of the gneissic and mica-schist systems, by the abrasion of the granite, and the gradual deposition of the detached matter at the bottom of the ocean, must have required a period, with the vastness of which the mind can hardly grapple, though perfectly insignificant in His view, to whom "one day is as a thousand years, and a thousand years are as one day." Of these two groups, Dr. Macculloch remarks, " The thickness of these strata we know to be enormous, their depths are discovered by geological observations and inferences —that they extend to many miles was also proved.—We have every reason to know, from what is now taking place on our own earth, that the accumulation of materials at the bottom of the ocean, is a work infinitely slow. We are sure that such an accumulation as should produce the primary strata as we now see them, must have occupied a space, from the contemplation of which the mind shrinks.*

The silurian rocks underlay the old red sandstone of England, and these are also estimated *at 3,000 yards in thickness.* The slate rocks of Scotland are several miles in thickness, and all exhibit the marks of slow deposition and subsequent consolidation. "We have traced," says the late Dr. James Douglas, of Glasgow, "a continuous 'out crop' of these rocks along the coast of Argyle for seven miles, and this is not one-third part of its extent. The whole slate or schistose formations of the west Highlands of Scotland generally 'crop out' in a north-west direction, and lie in an angle of from 45 to 70 or 80 degrees. They extend from about five miles below Dunoon, along the whole

---

* There are seven *distinct* geological *epochs* — each characterized by sedimentary deposits of enormous thickness, and each the work of thousands, if not millions of years.

coasts of Loch Long, and Loch Lomond, with nearly the same inclination. The slate rocks of England underlaying the silurian* system, are also of immense thickness. These facts show that, *previous to the carboniferous or coal era, when the earth began to be adorned with vegetation, myriads of ages must have passed away.*"

The carboniferous† formation excluding the mountain limestone, and millstone grit,‡ measures 1900 *yards in thickness.* Many of the limestones in this formation consist almost entirely of *organic* remains. Beds of limestone, 30 feet thick, and totally composed of zoophytes§ and shells of various kinds, are common in this formation : almost all *the sandstones contain the stems of trees belonging to genera or species now unknown, and many of the clays abound with the most delicate impressions of the fronds and leaves of ferns, and other plants most delicately preserved :* and fishes of enormous size are frequently met with.‖ Coal itself *is now universally acknowledged to be of vegetable origin.* The laminated nature of many of

---

* *Silurian*—from *Silures,* the name of the ancient inhabitants of Wales. The term Silurian is given to those rocks which occured between the clay slate and the carboniferous system

† *Carboniferous,* containing coal.

‡ *Millstone grit.* a series of rocks in England, which lie between the mountain limestone and the coal measures, as the beds are called, which contain workable seams of coal.

§ *Zoophite,* a coral or animal plant.

‖ Fishes make their first appearance in the upper beds of the Silurian rocks, but it is in the old red sandstone, where, on account of their extraordinary and well-developed forms, the study of them becomes definite and deeply interesting "No two mineral formations contain the same fishes, the species in each being quite distinct from those of another. With what interest then, must we regard these—the first—created of the many thousands of species which, since the period of the old red sandstone, *have moved through the waters of the ocean,* preying on each other, and otherwise performing the offices for which they were adapted by their peculiar organizations in the economy of Nature "—*Agassiz.*

the sandstones, and of the shale or slaty clays, *and their being frequently impressed with the ripple marks of the ancient waves, show that almost the whole of this immense mass of deposition was accumulated under the influence of comparatively tranquil water ;* if so, how amazing must the time have been during which these deposits were formed !

The roofs of some of the coal-beds exhibit great beauty of appearance, and a vast profusion of plants. " The finest example I ever witnessed," says the Rev. Dr. Buckland, "is that of the coal mines of Bohemia. The most elaborate imitations of living foilage upon the painted ceilings of Italian palaces bear no comparison with the beauteous profusion of external vegetable forms with which the galleries of these instructive mines are overhung. The roof is covered with a canopy of gorgeous tapestry, enriched with festoons of most graceful foilage, hung in wild irregular profusion over every portion of its surface. The effect is heightened by the contrast of the black color of these vegetables with the light ground of the rock to which they are attached. The spectator feels himself transported, as if by enchantment, into the forests of another world,

" So wondrous wild, the whole might seem
The scenery of a fairy dream ;"

he beholds trees of forms and characters now unknown upon the surface of the earth, presented to his senses almost in the beauty and vigor of their primeval life; their scaly stems and bending branches, with their delicate apparatus of foilage, all spread before him, little impaired by the lapse of countless ages, and bearing fruitful records of extinct systems of vegetation, which began and terminated in times of which these relics are the infallible historians."*

---

* The plants, which occur in the manner so beautifully described by the Doctor, are generally not in direct contact with the coal-bed, but at a little distance above it.

Advancing upwards until we arrrive at the sands of the ancient Triassic ocean—the saliferous,* or new red sandstone formation, we behold appearances as unexpected and startling, as the human footstep to Crusoe on his desolate island—the tracks of bipeds—colossal birds—of which no other vestiges remain, and to which the existing order of creation affords no parallel. Tracks of this description were found, in 1828, on new red sandstone, in the quarry of Corn Cockle Muir, in Dumfrieshire, at a depth of forty-five feet. After removing a large slab which presented footprints, perhaps the very next stratum, at a distance of a few feet or inches, exhibited the same phenomenon. Hence the process by which the impressions were made on the sand, and subsequently buried, must have been repeated at successive intervals. In another quarry in similar strata, near the town of Dumfries, the same marks were discovered, and in one instance a track extended from twenty to thirty feet in length. Dr. Buckland refers these impressions to land tortoises. In 1834, an account was published of some remarkable footsteps in the new red sandstone at Hesseburg, near Kildberghausen, in Saxony, at a depth of sixty-nine feet. The largest track appears to have been made by an animal whose hind foot was eight inches long. It has received the name of *Chirotherium*, from Professor Kaup, owing to the resemblance of its impressions to the shape of the human hand; but some of the tracks appear to have been made by tortoises, and M. Link suggests, that others are to be referred to gigantic batrachians, or frogs and salamanders.

The new red sandstone overlies the coal: it is about 9000 *feet in thickness* and yields evidence of similar conditions in the medium of deposition, as in the old red sandstone period. It contains besides red and variegated sandstones, marl† and conglomerates, immense beds of rock-salt, and

---

* *Saliferous*, containing salt.   † *Marl*, a compound of clay and lime.

layers of gypsum (sulphate of lime); it is in this series of
rocks where the saurian or crocodile tribe are first found.
The shells in it are all of marine origin.

The Lias* formation is superimposed upon the new red sandstone : it consists principally of limestone and shale, abound-
ing with a vast profusion of organic remains, differing in
species from any found in the older rocks.

A small slab of marl from Aix, in Provence, in the collection of R. J. Murchison, Esq., contains scores of small
fishes, as perfect as if recently imbedded in soft mud   In the
chalk formation, many of the fishes are uncompressed, the
body being as perfect in form as if the original had been
surrounded by soft plaster of Paris while floating in the
water.   But in coarse limestones and conglomerates, in other words, in materials that have been subjected to the action
of the waves, and torrents, detached teeth, scales, bones, &c.,
constitute the principal vestiges of this class of beings.

---

* *Lias*, a provincial word, meaning layers

CHAPTER III.

"To discover order and intelligence, in scenes of apparent wildness and confusion, is the pleasing task of the geological inquirer.—*Dr. Paris*

The next formation is the oolite,* consisting also of lime-stone and shales, and like the lias formation, teeming with the evidence of *a very different animal economy existing in the ancient from the modern ocean.* Among these are the remains of the Ichthyosaurus† and the Plesiosaurus,‡ animals *combining the structure of a fish with that of the crocodile,* and furnished with paddles like those of the whale. The character of these and the other animals will now be described, and from which the reader will perceive that time *must* have been required for their production and growth, *and that any condition of the ocean, by which deposition would be more hastily precipitated than now, would have been incompatible with the duration of their existence in the ancient seas.*

The periods of secondary deposition were those in which the Saurian tribe seemed to have attained the most extraor-dinary development, and many of them were formed after types which have *no analogy among existing forms ;* such are the flying Saurians, the Pterodactyles (fig. 4), the Ich-thyosaurians (fig. 1), and the Plesiosaurians (fig. 2). The highest of all the Iguanoden (fig. 6) has its representative in the recent Iguana ; the megalosaurus combined the struc-

---

* *Oolite,* from *oon,* an egg, and *lithos,* a stone, given to this formation from some of its limestones, containing little round particles like the roe of a fish.

† *Ichthyosaurus — ichthys,* a fish, and *saurus,* a lizard —(See fig. I.)

‡ *Plesiosaurus,* from *plesios* nearly allied, and *saurus,* a lizard.—(See fig. 2.)

ture of the living crocodile and moniter, while the Steneo-
saurus and the Teleosaurus, approached in the structure of
their heads and dental system, to the long-snouted Gavial,
the crocodile of the Ganges, while the Hylæosaurus, combined in its osteology the structure of the crocodile with
that of lizards armed with dorsal spinal ridges. These,
and all others yet discovered in rocks ranging from the
older deposits of the new red sandstone to the terminating
of the chalk formation, are all essentially distinct from
species now in existence, and form in our museums most
tangible evidences of the very different conditions of these
parts o the earth at the time when they crawled upon the
land, or swam in the water, or winged their flight through
the air. A brief notice of these tenants of the ancient
world is all our limits will afford.

*Ichthyosaurus** (Fig. 1.)—Ten species of this genus have
been found in the oolite and lias formation, varying considerably in size, the largest measuring *thirty feet in length.*
"In its general outline," says Dr. Buckland, "the ichthyosaurus must have most nearly resembled the modern porpoise and grampus. The animal was furnished with four
paddles, the front ones attached to a sternal arch of great
strength, and in a manner admirably adapted to the habits
of a creature requiring rapid motion through the ocean.
A similar construction of the sternum (breastbone) is only
met with among existing animals in that of the ornithorhynchus, or duck-billed water mole of New South Wales.
The snout resembled that of the porpoise; the teeth were
numerous, sharp and conical like those of a crocodile;

---

* The remains of these animals are found through the oolite, and in
the lower beds of the chalk formations, but the lias is especially their
sepulchre. They occur in great abundance in England, at Barrow-on-
Soar, in Leicestershire, in the valley of the Avon, between Bath and Bristol, and on the coast of Dorsetshire, where the cliffs appear to be inex-
haustible quarries of them —*Milner.*

the construction of the head was that of a lizard, with enormously large eyes; the vertebræ were doubly concave, like those of fishes, thus combining in its osteology the conformation of the whale, the ornithorhynchus, the crocodile, and a fish."

Fig. 1.

Ichthyosaurus communis.

Dr. Buckland in his Bridgewater Treatise mentions that the skeleton of one of these animals from Lyme Regis in Dorsetshire, preserved in the Oxford Musuem, contains within the ribs a large mass of undigested fish scales, which it had devoured previous to its death, and as this mass of coprolitic matter occurs through the entire region of the ribs, he concludes that like existing crocodiles, it must have had a capacious stomach, whole human bodies having been sometimes found in the latter. "The coprolites (dungstones) voided by Ichthyosauri, containing the bones, scales, and teeth, of the animals they fed on, are found in great abundance in the lias formation. At Lyme Regis, these coprolites are so abundant, *that they lie in some parts of the lias like potatoes scattered on the ground*; still more common are they in the estuary of the Severn, *where they are similarly disposed in strata of many miles in extent, and mixed up so abundantly with teeth and rolled fragments of the bones of reptiles and fishes, as to show that this region, having been the bottom of an ancient sea, was for a long period the receptacle of the bones and fæcal remains of its inhabitants.* Thus when we see the body of an Ichthyosaurus still containing the food it had eaten, just before its death, and its ribs still surrounding the remains of fishes that were swallowed ten thousand times ten thousand years ago, all these intervals seem annihilated, time altogether disappears, and we are brought into the imme- -diate contact with events of immeasurably distant periods as with the affairs of yesterday."

Plesiosaurus (Fig. 2).—This Enaliosaurian or fish-lizard, resembled the Ichthyosaurus in its being furnished with four paddles, in the concave structure of its vertrebæ, and in possessing the head of a lizard, and the teeth of a croco- dile; but its neck was enormously long, while its trunk and tail possessed the proportions of an ordinary quadruped. The head was comparatively small, the teeth conical, very slender, and curved inwards. Professor Owen enumerates not less than sixteen' species, some of which are *thirty feet in length*. In treating of this, perhaps the most hetroclitic of all animals, living or extinct, Conybeare observes:— " That it was aquatic is evident, from the form of its pad- dles—that it was marine, is almost equally so, from the re- mains with which it is universally associated — that it may have occasionully visited the shore, the resemblance of its extremities to those of the turtle, may lead us to conjecture;

Fig. 2.

Plesiosaurus.

its motions, however, must have been very awkward on land; its long neck must have impeded its progress through the water, presenting a striking contrast to the organization which so admirably fits the Ichthyosaurus to cut through the waves. May it not, therefore, be concluded, (since, in addition to these circumstances, its respiration must have required frequent access of air,) that it swam upon, or near the surface, arching its long neck like the swan, and occa- sionally darting it down at the fish which happened to float

within its reach. It may, perhaps, have lurked in shoal
water along the coast, concealed among the sea-weed, and
raising its nostrils to the surface from a considerable depth,
have found a secure retreat from the assaults of dangerous
enemies, while the length and flexibility of its neck may
have compensated for the want of strength in its jaws, and
its incapacity for swift motion through the water, by the
suddenness and agility of the attack which they enabled it
to make on every animal fitted for its prey which came within
reach."

*Megalosaurus.**—Remains of this crocodelian have been
found in the oolite at Stonesfield, in Oxfordshire, and at Be-
sancon, and also by Dr. Mantell, in the Wealden of Tilgate forest. From the size and nature of the bones found,
Cuvier considered the animal as partaking of the structure
of the moniter and crocodile, and to have been from *forty to
fifty feet in length*. The femur and tibia measure nearly
three feet each, so that the hind leg must have been about
six feet long. The thigh and leg bones of crocodiles, and
other aquatic quadrupeds, are solid throughout, but those of
the Megalosaurus were hollow, like those of land quadrupeds,—an arrangement by which both lightness and strength
are secured. It is therefore conjectured, that the Saurian,
under consideration, lived chiefly on land. The structure
of its serrated teeth indicate it to have been carnivorous.

Fig. 3.

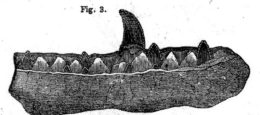

Anterior extremity of the right lower jaw of Megalosaurus in side
view one fourth of nat. size.

---

* From μεγας, great, and σαῦρος, a lizard.

*Pterodactyle** (fig. 4).—The extinct reptiles denominated *Pterodactyles,* are unquestionably the most marvelous even

Fig. 4.

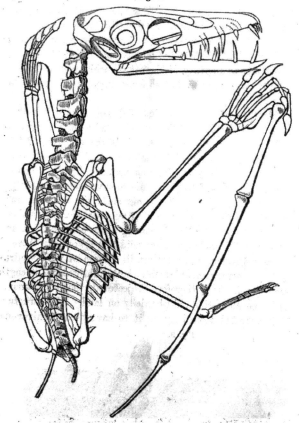

Pterodactylus Crassirostris (restored by Goldfuss).

of the wonderful beings which the relics of the Age of Rep-

* πτερὸν *a wing,* and δάμντυλος, *a finger.*

tiles have enabled the palæontologist to reconstruct, and
place before us in their natural forms and appearance.
With a head and length of neck resembling those of a bird,
the wings of a vampire or bat, and the body and tail of an
ordinary mammalian, these creatures present an anomaly of
structure as unlike their fossil contemporaries, as is the duck-
billed Platypus, or Ornithorhynchus, of Australia, the existing animals. The skull is small, with very long beaks,
which extend like those of the crocodile, and are furnished
with upward of sixty sharp, pointed teeth; the eyes were
enormous, enabling the creature to fly by night. The fore-
finger is immensely elongated, for the support of a membra-
nous expansion, as in the bat : the impression of the wing-
membrane is preserved on the stone in some examples; and
the fingers terminated, as in that animal, in long curved
claws. The size and form of the foot, leg, and thigh, show
that the *Pterodactyles* were capable of perching on trees,
and of standing firmly on the ground. when, with its wings

Fig. 5.

Restorations of Saurians and other animals of the Lias.

folded, it might walk or hop like a bird. Dr. Buckland is
of opinion that it had the power of swimming. Fig. 5 exhibits the chief reptiles of the Liassic age, the Ichthyosaurus and Plesiosaurus; the latter in the act of catching a
pterodactyle.

> " With head uplift above the waves, and eyes
> That sparkling blazed, his other parts besides,
> Prone on the flood, extended long and large,
> Lay floating many a rood, in bulk as huge
> As whom the fables name of monstrous size,
> Titanian, or earth-born, that warred on Jove.
> Briarchus, or Typhon, whom the den
> By ancient Tarsus held, or that sea beast
> Leviathan, which God of all his works
> Created hugest that swam the ocean stream "

Cuvier in his great work, pronounces these flying reptiles
the most extraordinary of all the beings whose ancient existence is revealed to us; and those which, if alive, would
seem most at variance with living forms. Eight species
have been-determined, from the size of a snipe to that of a
cormorant, occurring in the lias of Lyme Regis, the oolite
of Stonesfield, the grit of the Wealden, and on the continent
at Pappenheim and Solenhofen.

With flocks of such like creatures flying in the air, and
shoals of no less monstrous Ichthyosauri and Plesiosauri
swarming in the ocean, and gigantic crocodiles and tortoises
crawling on the shores

> " Till all the plume-dark air
> And rude resounding shore are one wild cry "—

of the primeval lakes and rivers; air, sea, and land, must
have been strangely peopled in those early periods of our
infant world.

CHAPTER IV.

"Mighty Pre-Adamites who walk'd the earth,
Of which ours is the wreck."

HYLÆOSAURUS'(Weald Lizard).—The lizard thus denominated by the discoverer, Dr. Mantell, was about *twenty-five feet in length,* and is chiefly remarkable by a large spiny process along the back, which must have given to such a creature a terrific appearance. Such process is found in many of the living lizards.

Iguanodon (fig. 6).—The remains of this, the most gigantic of all reptiles living or extinct, were also made known to the world by Dr. Mantell. The bones obtained by the doctor indicate the existence of a herbivorous lizard,

Fig. 6.

The Iguanodon.

allied in structure to the iguana of the West Indies ; *seven-ty feet in length,* and *fourteen and a half feet in circumfer-ance round the body.* A thigh bone measures *three feet eight inches, and thirty-five inches in circumference,* and the bones of the foot show it to have been *six and a half feet in length.* The nose of the animal was armed with a horn, equal in size, and resembling in form, the lesser horn upon the nose of the rhinoceros, — an apparatus which also exists on the nose of the iguana. The teeth, some of which are two and a half inches in length, are deeply serrated, and their resemblance to those of the iguana, clearly demonstrate that, like it, it was of herbivorous habits. Besides the re-mains found in Tilgate Forest, in strata of the Wealden formation, Dr. Mantell mentions the discovery of another at Maidstone, in an arenaceous or sandy limestone, called Kentish rag, belonging to the Shanklin sands. This rock, he observes, abounds in the marine shells, which are char-acteristic of that division of the chalk formation. In the quarry in which the remains of this iguanodon were found, Mr. Benson has discovered fossil wood by the boring shells, the lithodomi ; impressions of leaves, stems of trees, ammon-ites, nautili, &c., large conical striated teeth, which are re-ferrible to those extinct fossil fishes which M. Agassiz de-nominates sauroid, or lizard-like, scales and teeth of several kinds of fishes, and among these a jaw or mandible of that singular genus of fish, the Chimera.

The geological position of this specimen forms an excep-tion to what has been previously remarked of the fossils of the Wealden ; for, while the bones in the latter were asso-ciated with terrestrial and fluviatile remains, only the Maid-stone specimen is imbedded in a marine deposit. This dis-crepancy nowise affects the arguments as to the fluviatile origin of the Wealden ; *it merely shows that part of the delta had subsided, and was covered by the chalk ocean, while the country of the iguanodon was still in existence.*

*The body of the iguanodon was then driven out to sea, and
became imbedded in the sand of. the ocean ; in the like
manner, as at the present day, bones of land quadrupeds
may not only be engulphed in deltas, but also in the deposits of the adjacent sea.*

The oolite is succeeded by the Wealden, green sand and
chalk formations measuring 660 yards in thickness, and containing immense quantities of fresh water and marine remains, the species being almost all different from those in
the older rocks, and none of them occurring in the newer.
The Wealden is one of estuary origin, containing many
fresh water shells, and the bones of enormous reptiles : one
of which, the iguanodon, must have measured *seventy feet
from snout to tail,* and been *fourteen feet in girth round
the body.* The chalk and green sand abound with marine
remains. It appears certain that the beds of this wonderful
formation add to the antiquity of the earth. Come when
the solution may, there is little likelihood of it shortening,
but every probability of it extending the period that has
elapsed since God called into existence the " heavens and the
earth."

The chalk is succeeded by the tertiary deposits, in which
the existing species make their first appearance. In the
lower or first of the tertiary formations, there are only about
five per cent. of existing marine shells; in the second, or
middle formation, the number of recent and extinct species
is nearly equal ; in the last, or newest of these deposits, the

* Let the reader visit the British Museum, and after examining the largest thigh-bone of the Iguanodon, repair to the Zoological Gallery, and
inspect the recent Crocodilian reptiles, some twenty-five or thirty feet in
length; and observe that the fossil bone equals, if not surpasses, in size
the entire thigh of the largest of existing reptiles , then let him imagine this
bone clothed with proportionate muscles and integuments, and reflect
upon the enormous trunk which such limbs must have been destined to
move and to sustain, and he will obtain a just notion of the appaling magnitude of the lizards which inhabited the country of the Iguanodon.

recent shells amount to ninety-five per cent.—*circumstan-ces which show a gradual increase of marine animal life, for a long series of ages previous to our historical epoch.* The tertiary rocks in the neighborhood of Paris, and other places, abound with the remains of extinct quadrupeds allied to the tapirs with the bones of elephants, rhinoceroses, hip-popotami, lions, tigers, and many other animals belonging to existing genera, but of different species from any now living. The teeth and bones of horses are often met with in the elephant bed, in Brighton cliffs; they are referable to a small species, about the size of a Shetland pony.*

> "Yes! where the huntsman winds his matin horn.
> And the couch'd hare beneath the covert trembles;
> Where shepherds tend their flocks, and grows the corn;
> Where Fashion on our gay Parade assembles—
> Wild Horses, Deer, and Elephants have strayed,
> Treading beneath their feet old Ocean's races."

Megatherium, (Fig 7.)—This leviathan of the vast plains

Fig. 7.

Skeleton of the Megatherium.

* The bones of the Kangaroo have been also found in England. That the remains of an extinct species of gigantic *Kangaroo* should be found

of South America, which were once occupied by immense
numbers of the race now entirely extinct, partakes of the
generic character of the existing diminutive sloths.   It ri-
valled in size the largest rhinoceros, was armed with claws
of enormous length and power, its whole frame possessing
an extreme degree of solidity.   With a head and neck like
those of the sloth, its legs and feet exhibit the character of
the armadillo and the ant-eater.   Some specimens of the
animal give the measurement of five feet across the haunches,
and the thigh bone was nearly three times as thick as that
of the elephant.   The spinal marrow must have been a foot
in diameter, and the tail, at the part nearest the body, twice
as large, or six feet in circumference.   The girth of the
body was fourteen feet and a half, and the length eighteen
feet.   The teeth were admirably adapted for cutting vegetable substances, and the general structure and strength of
the frame for tearing up the ground in search of roots,
wrenching off the branches of trees, and uprooting their
trunks, on which it principally fed.   "Heavily constructed,
and ponderously accoutred," says Dr. Buckland, in his elo-
quent description of the megatherium, "it could neither
run, nor leap, nor climb, nor burrow under the ground;
and all its movements must have been necessarily slow.
But what need of rapid locomotion to an animal whose occupation, of digging roots for food, was almost stationary?
And what need of speed for flight from foes, to a creature
whose giant carcase was encased in an impenetrable cuirass,
and who, by a single pat of his paw, or lash of his tail,
could in an instant have demolished the couguar or the

---

in the fissures of the rocks, and in the caverns of Australia, a country in
which marsupial animals are the principal existing mammalia, is a fact
that will not excite much surprise; but that beings of this remarkable
type of organization should ever have inhabited the countries situated in
the latitude of the European continent and of Great Britain, would never
have been suspected, but for the researches of the geologist.

crocodile? Secure within the panoply of his strong ar-
mour, where was the enemy that would dare encounter this
leviathan of the Pampas? or in what more powerful creature can we find the cause that has effected the extirpation
of his race? His entire frame was an apparatus of colossal
mechanism, adapted exactly to the work it had to do.
Strong and ponderous in proportion as this work was heavy
and calculated to be the vehicle of life and enjoyment to a
gigantic race of quadrupeds, which, though they have ceased
to be counted among the living inhabitants of our planet,
have in their fossil bones left behind them imperishable
monuments of the consummate skill with which they were
constructed."

The oolite quarries of Portland have been long remarkable for their containing certain strata called the "dirt-
beds," in which the stems and branches of coniferous trees
and cycadeæ* are found in considerable abundance. Many
of the trees as well as the plants are still erect (see Fig 8.),
with their roots ramified in the dirt-beds, which appears to
be the soil in which they grew. "On my visit," says Dr.
Mantell, "to the island in the summer of 1832, the surface
of a large area of the dirt-bed was cleared, preparatory to
its removal, and a most striking phenomenon was presented
to my view. The floor of the quarry was literally strewed
with fossil wood, and I saw before me *a petrified tropical
forest;* the trees and plants like the inhabitants of the Alg,
in the Arabian story, being converted into stone, yet still
maintaining their place, which they occupied when alive!
Some of the trunks were surrounded by a conical mound of
calcareous matter, which had evidently once been earth, and
had accumulated around the base and roots of the trees.
The stems were generally three or four feet high, their
summits being jagged and splintered, as if they had been

---

* A genus of plants allied to the palms and ferns.

corn and wrenched off by a *hurricane*—an appearance which many trees in this neighborhood (Bristol) after the late storm, strikingly resembled. Some of the trunks were two feet in diameter, and the united fragments of one tree measured upwards of thirty feet in length; in other specimens, branches were attached to the stem. In the dirt-bed there were many trunks lying prostrate, and fragments of branches. The fossil plants are called Cycadeodia, by Dr. Buckland, from their analogy to the recent Cycas and Zamia, but for which M. Adolphe Brongniart has established a new genus, named Mantellia. The plants occurred at intervals between the trees, and the dirt-bed was so little consolidated, that I dug up with a spade, as from a floor, several specimens that must have been on the very spot on which they grew, like the columns of Puzzioli, preserved erect amidst all the revolutions which the surface of the earth have subsequently undergone, and beneath the accumulated spoils of numberless ages. The trees and plants are completely petrified by silex or flint."

From what has been stated, it is evident, that after the marine strata, forming the base of the isle of Portland, *were deposited at the bottom of a deep sea, and had become consolidated, the bed of that ancient ocean was elevated above the level of the waters, became dry land, and was covered by forests.* How long this new country existed cannot now be ascertained; but that it flourished for a considerable period is certain, from the number and magnitude of the trees of the petrified forest. In the isle of Purbeck, traces of the dirt-bed, with trunks of trees, are seen beneath the fresh water limestone of the Weald; a proof that, *before the deposition of the Purbeck marble could have taken place,* the petrified forest must have sunk to the depth of many hundred feet.

Space will not permit us to describe the other varieties of the vegetable kingdom which occur in secondary strata;

it must therefore suffice to observe, that like their contemporary animals, they are all more or less indicative of a much higher temperature than is now enjoyed in the latitudes in which they occur.

Fig. 8.

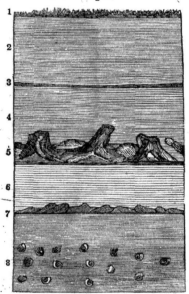

1, Vegetable soil. 2, 4, and 6, Fresh water limestone. 3, Clay. 5 and 7, Dirt-bed with Cycadites, &c. 8, Portland oolite containing marine shells, &c.

In none of these formations have the remains of *man* or of his works been ever found.

The facts that have been stated, will, we think, satisfy the reader of the justness of the conclusion, *that the whole stratified rocks which constitute the crust of the earth are derived from matter deposited by water at the bottom of the sea, in estuaries or lakes which at the time were inhabited by animals differing in species and genera from any*

that now exist; and that consequently, the present struc-
ture and configuration of the earth is the offspring of a
vast antiquity. Of the myriads of living creatures, that

"The earth has gathered to her breast again,"

how few, comparatively, could even the transcendent genius
of Cuvier reveal! Finding, even in these restricted bounds,
the amplest proof of order and design, the mind is naturally
led to the sublimest inferences respecting what is unseen,
and even to the conception of a power and intelligence to
which we may well apply the term *infinite;* since we not
only see no limit to the instances in which they are mani-
fested, but find, on the contrary, that they continually open
upon us in increasing abundance, in proportion as we are
enabled to extend our sphere of observation and inquiry,
and that as the study of one prepares us to understand and
appreciate another, wonder follows on wonder, till our faculties become bewildered in admiration, and our intellect
falls back on itself in utter hopelessness of arriving at an
end.

In the tertiary rocks, the number of species of fossil
shells found is 2728. In the chalk rocks 500 — in the
oolite 771 — in the new red sandstone 118 — in the carboniferous rocks 336, and in the silurian and greywacke*
systems 349 ; making in all, 4832 different species. The
greater proportion of these are as perfect in their structure
as the living species.

Such are the views of modern geologists with respect to
the age of our earth. Unfolding as they do the most evident traces of the continued exercise of the creative power,
in the production of creatures from time to time fitted to
the existing physical conditions of the globe; they offer

---

* *Greywacke,* a name given to an indurated sandstone, belonging to
the slate rocks.

incontrovertible testimony to the existence of an infinitely intelligent and all-powerful *First Cause*, and thus lay the foundation of a true knowledge of the great Architect of the universe.

CHAPTER V.

GENERAL REMARKS ON THE DIFFERENT FORMATIONS.

HAVING enumerated and briefly described nearly all the stratified formations that are known to occur in the crust of the earth, we proceed to make some general remarks, founded upon the facts that have passed before us. Let it be distinctly understood, that the object of these remarks is to prove, on geological grounds, the greater antiquity of the earth than that generally assigned to it .

The first argument in favor of the antiquity of the globe, is founded on the *number of strata that go to make up its crust.* The crust of the earth, or that rocky band that surrounds and encloses *its molten contents,* is about *ten miles thick.* The greater part of this mass has been examined, nature having laid open or tilted up almost all the formations of which it is composed. To accomplish this apparently impossible task, the geologist has but to walk over the uplands, ascend the river beds,

> " To sit on rocks, to muse o'er flood and fell,
> To slowly trace the forest's shady scene,
> Where things that own not man's dominion dwell,
> And mortal foot hath ne'er or rarely been;
> To climb the trackless mountain all unseen,
> With the wild flock that never needs a fold;
> Alone o'er steeps and foaming falls to lean;
> This is not solitude; 'tis but to hold
> Converse with Nature's charms, and view her stores
>   unroll'd,"

penetrate the gloomy ravines, and climb the mountain ridges. In this way all those formations enumerated in preceding chapters, have been examined by those who make nature their study.

At present we leave out of view the granite and other igneous rocks; also the metamorphic rocks, namely, gneiss, mica-schist, and clay-slate. The number of distinct beds above these is no less than *fifty-seven*, many of which are several hundred feet thick. Of course these beds do not occur in a regular series one above the other; were this the case, the crust of the earth would resemble the concentric layers of an onion, and would be much beyond ten miles thick. They lie in patch-like masses; generally speaking, the more ancient are the most extensive, and the more recent the most circumscribed. *All these beds bear distinct evidence of their formation under water.* This cannot be disputed, if we are to take present nature for our guide. The rocks of these ancient seas, lakes, and rivers, present the same appearances at this distant date, that are observed in estuaries, the margins of lakes, and the shores of the ocean at the present day.— The fine mud is seen in thin layers as it originally subsided to the bottom of the waters. *The sandstones bear the impress of the receding wave on the ancient sea-beach.* Nay, the surface of the beds are sometimes *pitted with the heavy rain-drops that have fallen upon them,* when yet expanses of loose sand, and exposed to the weather.

It is not more certain that these stratified rocks are of *aqueous* origin, than that the various formations have been deposited in succession. The evidence of this remark will be more fully brought out in illustrating points that are not yet referred to. Meanwhile, it may suffice to state, that this is proved both from the mineralogical character of the formations, and their fossil contents. Not only is this true of the various formations, or groups of strata; as a general principle it is also true of the members of these formations. These *fifty-seven* beds are not simply proved to be of *aque-*

ous origin, *but also to have been deposited in succession.*
The same rock, or its equivalent, in other parts of the
world, would be deposited during or about the same period;
but this was not the case with rocks whose positions in the
scale were apart from each other. To illustrate this: The
British chalk beds, and their foreign equivalents, were deposited during the same period; but the upper chalk, and
the London clay, were deposited in succession.

That this long series of rocks occupied *numerous ages
in·accumulating,* is obvious, first, from the fact, *that many
of them are of enormous thickness.* Secondly, each group
required for its perfection, at least two (in many instances
a greater number) changes of land and water. Now judg-
ing from the operations of nature in the historic period, we
may conclude that these changes were gradual ; and if gradual—indeed many of the rocks bear internal evidence to the
fact—who can reckon the time consumed in their formation ?

The second argument in favor of the antiquity of the
globe, is drawn from *the nature of the strata,* or their mineralogical character. Under this argument we do not in-
clude those rocks that are composed, to any extent, of organic remains; their proper place is in connection with the
next. The rocks of which we now speak, namely, the coarse
and fine sandstones—the beds of shale, marl, clay, slates,
&c , are composed of older rocks. Let us take the old·red
sandstone as an example. The conglomerate, so largely developed in this system, is not a rock composed of new materials; the geologist recognises the pebbles of which it is
almost entirely made up, as belonging to rocks lower in the
series. And the finer beds that accompany and overlie the
conglomerate, are obviously, in many instances, composed of
the same material ground into small particles. These illus-
trations apply to the whole class of rocks of which we are now
treating. The material of which they are composed, whether

in its present combination in the shape of shale, clay, flags, or sandstone, has, in every instance, been associated with, or constituted entirely, the rocks that precede each other in the series.

These remarks raise several questions, each of which leads us to draw largely upon time. Before the great conglomerate, the lowest member of the old red sandstone, was deposited, the pebbles of which it is principally composed must have existed in the shape of quartz rock in beds or masses; and truly they must have occupied large areas of the surface of the earth as it then was. These masses must have been broken up into fragments of all sizes, probably by internal commotions, aided by the influence of water.

The conglomerates deposited, we must find time for the formation of the sandstone. The beds of this rock are often very thick, and are exceedingly numerous. The matter of which they are composed originally existed as rock, *and through long exposure to the atmosphere, the showers of heaven, the continuing ripple of running water, and the incessant beat of the ocean wave, it has been disengaged from its original combinations, carried downward to the ocean, and after being held for a time in mechanical or chemical solution by the water, is spread out upon its bottom.* This is not the work of a few years. But how are the demands upon time increased, when we reflect that rocks thus formed by slow degrees, are consolidated, heaved upward, exposed to the elements, and by partial decay supply the material for beds higher in the series, and which pass through the same tedious processes in their formation?

Perhaps the immense beds of shale, and clay, that intermingle with the harder rocks, required a period to accumulate, little short of that which *must* be granted to the sandstones. The material of which they are composed has also been supplied by mechanical and chemical causes, and, in course of time, accumulated to the extent we find them developed in the various formations.

The mineralogical character of the rocks, then, unquestionably prove their formation to have been slow, and continued over a period of time to us immeasurable.

The third argument in favor of the antiquity of the globe is drawn from *the fossil contents of the strata.* The strata enumerated are more or less fossiliferous; very few of them are entirely destitute of organic remains. *In the older rocks we have fishes, shells, and plants: in the more recent, shells in greater abundance, plants in large quantities, and bones of quadrupeds and birds, are associated with the impressions and skeletons of fishes.* The presence of these remains and the nature of them, lead us to assign a much longer period for the depositing of the rocks in which they occur, than is generally allowed.

There are fishes of all sizes and various ages; and like the fishes in the present seas, they must have acquired time to arrive at maturity. The position in which they are frequently found, when their stony matrix is opened, *indicates that they have sunk in the mud of the sea-bottom, and been overlaid with newer sediment.* This was the work of time. And the time required for the depositing of *one fish formation*, must be multiplied by the number of such formations the crust of the earth contains. The same line of argument is applicable to the *fossil shells, plants, and bones* that are scattered so profusely throughout the strata.

In carrying out this argument we must refer to the fact that some rocks of the series are entirely, or in great part, composed *of animal or vegetable remains.* The coal is a familiar illustration. That this rock is composed of vegetable matter, is now universally acknowledged. In the sandstone and shales that occur in the coal beds, many plants, in fragments, are imbedded; *but when the coal is examined no doubt rests on the mind but that it is wholly composed*

4

plants and trees. By a lately invented process, this examination is carried on with great accuracy. The coal is
sliced into thin leaves, and placed under a powerful glass.
In this way the peculiar character of the stem under examination is at once recognised, *and the fact established that
the coal is of vegetable origin.* An obvious inference is
drawn from this fact. The growth of these plants and trees
required time ; and the produce of many generations was required to make up even a thin bed of coal, the collecting
and consolidating, therefore, of only one bed, must have
stretched over a long period. It may be granted that vegetation, during the epoch of the earth's history of which we
are now treating, was more rapid and luxuriant; still our
conclusion is not affected much thereby.

Some limestones are known to be composed almost entirely of organic remains. The *exuviæ* of creatures, all too
minute to be detected by the unaided eye, are collected in
such masses *as to furnish beds of rock many feet thick.*
It is superfluous to say, that the formation of *such* rocks
must have been the work of time. Again, it is well known
that corals enter largely into the composition of limestone.
In some instances, it would appear that the rock is one mass
of these zoophytes. Now, from all we have been able to
learn of the habits and modes of operation of these diminutive laborers, we are left to conclude, that the general progress
of the mass of calcareous matter which they secrete, is
slow. It has been calculated that the growth of six inches
requires a century.* Let the thickness of the beds, and the
number that occur in the earth's crust, be taken into account,
and we again find ourselves driven backward into an unknown antiquity.

In connexion with this argument, there is still another
point to which reference should, in justice, be made. The
fossils that exist in a given formation, are not identical with

---

* Williams' Missionary Enterprise in the South Sea Islands, p 9.

those that exist in the overlying group. They may, and do present resemblances, more or less near; but there is a change; and such a change as indicates that between the close of the one formation, and the opening of the other, a considerable period has elapsed. This remark is applicable to the formations of the palæozoic and secondary periods; hence each group has its characteristic fossils. It is also true in regard to the rocks of the tertiary period, viewed as groups. But it does not apply to the upper beds of the secondary, and lower beds of the tertiary formations. The time that transpired between the depositing of these, was such as, together with the changes that took place, to break the connexion entirely between the fossils of the one and those of the other. No species found in the chalk, the upper bed of the secondary formation, extends into the London clay, the lowest in the tertiary groups. There is here a break, of a much greater extent than those that appear to exist between each formation and its successor, of the older periods; and the length of time which it represents, though uncertain, must be great.

The only other argument produced in favor of the antiquity of the globe, is derived *from the relative position in which the various groups that compose the crust are placed.* Groups of rock either lie comformable or uncomformable upon each other. There are few that lie conformable, that is, as you would place one volume fair upon another. But even when this is the case, there are certain indications at the junction that demonstrate, *that the surface of the lower group was long consolidated, and exposed to the elements, before it was overlaid by the beds of the upper.* Thus, if we find the surface-rock partially decomposed and removed, what remains, hollowed out by water, and these *hollows* occasionally containing *loose* pebbles, we may reasonably conclude that these effects—the result of time—were produced before the overlying rock had been deposited.

O, how varied are the aspects this planet presents in the course of this vast revolution! The first certain glance we obtain presents to our view a world whose seas teemed with living inhabitants, chiefly of the fish tribes, of various size, of the most fantastic shapes, and of the most elegant colors. Perishable as the last quality is, we have seen rise, phœnix-like, from the plates or scales of one of these fossil fishes, under the influence of a powerful glass, in hues that rival those of the rainbow. Meanwhile, the land presents but a scanty vegetation, which may give shelter and support to living creatures, but none of which come within the sphere of our vision. Another turn, and the earth is clothed with a luxuriant and extensively distributed vegetation, resembling that of the tropics in the present time; while the seas and lakes swarm with shell and other fishes. We look again, and behold creatures of monstrous size, and singular conformation, basking on the banks of rivers, gamboling in the fenny pools, crawling on the moist earth, or floating through the air. Another glance, and the noble forests are seen to give shelter to quadrupeds, in comparison to which the largest of the present time appear dwarfish. These browse upon the leaves and tender sprouts, or burrow in the earth in search of roots. Still another glance, and these creatures are being replaced by others more nearly approaching the type of living creation.

In all this, there is the amplest evidence that the Creator of the "heaven and the earth" is great, and wise, and good. His power is felt in every change, His wisdom is manifest in every arrangement; and every plant, and tree, and creature, speaks of His goodness.

A GEOLOGICAL EXCURSION

TO

TILGATE FOREST, A. D. 2000.

BY THOMAS HOOD, ESQ , WITH EMENDATIONS AND ADDITIONS,

BY AN ANTIQUARIAN.

TIME has been called the test of truth, and some old verities have made him testy enough. Scores of ancient authorities has he exploded like Rupert's drops, by a blow upon their tails : but at the same time he has bleached many black-looking stories into white ones, and turned some tremendous bouncers into what the French call *accomplished facts*. Look at the Magatherium, which a century ago even credulity would have scouted! The headstrong fiction which Mrs. Malaprop treated as a mere allegory on the banks of the Nile, is now the *Iguanodon!* To venture a prophecy, there are more such prodigies to come true.

Suppose it a fine morning Anno Domini 2000, and the royal geologists, with Von Hammer at their head — pioneers, excavators, borers, trappists, greywackers, carbonari, field-sparrers, and what not, are marching to have a grand field-day in Tilgate Forest A good cover has been marked out for a find. Well! to work they go; hammer and tongs, banging, splitting, digging, shoveling, puffing like a smith's bellows — hot as his forge — dusty as millers — muddy as eels — what with sandstone and gritstone, and pudding-stone, blue clay and brown, marl and bog-

earth—now unsextonizing a petrified bachelor's button—
now a stone tom-tit—now a marble gooseberry-bush—
now one of St. Cuthbert's beads*—now a couple of Kentish cherries, all stone, turned into Scotch pebbles—now a
fossil red herring—now one of St. Patrick's petrified frogs.
But these are geological bagatelles! We want the organic
remains of one of Og's bulls, or Gog's hogs—that's the
Mastodon—or Magog's pet lizard, that's the *Iguanodon*—
or Polyphemu's elephant, that's the *Magatherium*. So in
they go again, with crash like Thor's Scandinavian hammer, and a touch of the earthquake, and lo! another and a
greater *Bony-part* to exhume! Huzza! shouts the field-
sparrer. Hold on, cries one, let go, shouts another—there
he comes, says a third—no, he don't, says a fourth. Where's
his nose?

What fatiguing work it is only to look at him, he's so
prodigious! There, there now, easy! Just hoist a bit—
a little, a little more. Pray, pray, pray take care of his
lumbar processes, they're very friable—Never you fear, zur
—if he be friable I'll ate 'em.

Bravo! there's his cranium—Is that brain, I wonder, or
mud? no, 'tis——! Now for the cervical vertebræ. Stop
—somebody hold his jaw. That's your sort! there's his
scapula. Now, then, dig, boys, dig, dig into his ribs. Work
away, lads—you shall have oceans of strong beer, and
mountains of bread and cheese, when you've got him out.
We can't be above a hundred yards from his tail! Huzza!
there's his ——!! I wish I could shout from here to Lon-

---

* They commonly occur singly in the northern counties, passing under
the denominations of "wheel-stones," and "St Cuthbert's beads," from
having been strung as beads, and formerly used as rosaries. Hence the
lines in Marmion :

> " On a rock by Lindisfern
> St. Cuthbert sits, and toils to frame
> The sea-born beads that bear his name."

don. There's his——!!! Work away, my good fellows—
never give up; we shall all go down to posterity. It's the
first—the first—the first nobody knows what—that's been
discovered in the world.

Here, lend me a spade, and I'll help. So, I'll tell you
what, we're all *Columbuses*, every man Jack of us! but I
can't dig—it breaks my back. Never mind: there he is
—and his tail with a broad arrow at the end! It's a *Hylæosaurus!* but no—that scapula's a wing—it's the Pterodactyle—by Saint George, it's a flying dragon.

, Huzza! shouts Boniface, the landlord of the village inn
that has the Saint George and the Dragon as his sign.

Huzza! echoes every Knight of the Garter.

Huzza! cries each schoolboy who has read the Seven
Champions.

Huzza, huzza! roar the illustrators of Schiller's Kampf
mit dem Drauchen.

Huzza, huzza, huzza! chorus the descendants of Moor of
Moor Hall.

. The legends *are* all true, then?

Not a bit of it! cries a stony-hearted professor of fossil
osteology. Look at the teeth, they're *all molar ;* he's a *My-
lodon!* That creature ate neither sheep, nor oxen, nor
children, nor tender virgins, nor hoary pilgrims, nor even
geese and turkeys—he lived on—

What? what? what? they all exclaim. Why, on raw
potatoes, and undressed salads, to-be-sure!

In Lucretius, we have a description of quadrupeds, recognized as existing previous to man and the present race of
animals, which might almost warrant the belief that some
fossil gigantic skeleton had met his eye:

> " Hence, doubtless, earth prodigious forms at first
> Gender'd, of face and members most grotesque ;
> Monsters,—half-man, half-woman—
> —shapes unsound,

Footless, and handless, void of mouth or eye,
Or, from misjunction, maim'd of limb with limb.
        —Many a tribe has sunk supprest,
Powerless its kind to gender."

APPENDIX.

ON THE

SCENERY IN Á PATCH OF INFINITE SPACE.*

(DEDUCED FROM AUTHENTIC SOURCES.)

"Now trace each orb with telescopic eyes,
And solve the eternal clock-work of the skies."

THE SUN AND SOLAR PHENOMENA OF OUR SYSTEM.—The sun—the central luminary of our system—the scource of light and heat—appears to prosecute daily a stately procession through the heavens, owing to the rotation of the earth upon its axis, ascending like an intensely brilliant ball from the eastern horizon, and declining towards the western. Excepting the regions bordering on the poles, every part of our globe, within the interval of twenty-four hours, is brought beneath the action of the solar rays, and withdrawn from them—its "mountains and all hills, its fruitful trees and all cedars." The unfailing continuity and nice precision with which this has transpired, age after age, strikingly illustrates the stability of the natural laws.

The decline of the sun to the horizon is as imposing a spectacle as his advance to it, when the atmosphere favors the exhibition of his descent. The most gorgeous sunsets are those of the West Indies, during the rainy season; the sky is then sublimely mantled with gigantic masses of clouds,

---

* Infinite space belongs to God, and to God alone. Infinite Power has filled that space with suns and systems, but there has been room for all.— *Professor Mitchell.*

which are tinged with the glare of the descending luminary,
and which seem to be impatiently waiting for his departure
in order to discharge their pent-up wrath on the bosom of
the night. In the South Atlantic the sunset has a milder
and more sober aspect. In the Eastern tropics it has generally an overpowering fierceness, as though the last expression of the solar heat should be the greatest. But during
the summer, in temperate latitudes there is often a serenely
beautiful horizon, a mellowness of light, together with a rich
and varied coloring on the sky, which combine to render the
European sunsets far more attractive than those which are
intertropical. The milder radiance of the "great light"
in parting from us presents a picture to the eye of the sentiment of the All-Merciful, "Again, a little while and ye
shall see me." And how open to observation are wise Contrivance and bountiful Design in the unvarying position of
the sun in the centre of our system, and the axical rotation
of his tributaries, which not only guarantee the regular
return of their surfaces to his presence, but the undimin-
ished power and splendor of his beams! If, adopting the
nebular hypothesis, we suppose the masses of the sun and of
the planets to have been gradually formed, under control of
the law of attraction, the question still arises, how it came
to pass, that the self-luminous matter was collected into one
mass at the centre, and not gathered into many masses like
the matter of the planets. So striking did this circumstance appear to Newton, that he remarked in his first letter to Bentley : "*I do not think it explicable by mere natural causes, but am forced to ascribe it to the counsel and
contrivance of a Voluntary Agent.*"

The mean distance of the sun from our earth, as determined by observation of the transit of Venus, is *ninety-five
millions of miles* ; and according to Laplace, this must be
within $\frac{1}{17}$ of the true distance, so that no error is involved
either way greater than about a million of miles. The im-

mense magnitude of the solar body appears from the fact that he occupies so much space in the heavens, and presents such a stately aspect, with so vast an interval between us. If a locomotive had been started five centuries and a half ago, and had been travelling incessantly at the rate of twenty miles an hour, it would only now have accomplished a space equal to that which lies between the terrestrial and the solar surface. Though light comes from the former to the latter in about *eight minutes*, a cannon ball would not perform the same feat, retaining its full force, under twenty-two years. That an object therefore should be so splendidly visible as the sun, so far removed, and should so powerfully influence us with light and heat, argues the stupendous dimensions of his volume. His direct light is supposed to be equal to that of 5570 *wax candles placed at the distance of one foot from an object*; and so great is the power of his rays, that some of the men employed in constructing the Plymouth Breakwater, had their caps burnt in a diving bell, *thirty feet under water*, owing to their sitting under the focal point of the convex glasses in the upper part of the machine. His real diameter of 882,000 miles is equal to 111¼ times that of our earth; and his circumference of 3,764,600 miles describes a bulk *nearly a million and a quarter times* larger than our globe, and above five hundred times greater than the united volume of all the planetary bodies of our system that revolve around him. If his mass occupied the place of the earth, it would fill up the entire orbit of our moon, and extend into space as far again as the path of that satellite. The density of the solar substance is, however, far less than that of the matter of our globe. If the two bodies could be weighed in a balance, the weight of the sun would not preponderate in the same proportion as his bulk, but be only 354,936 times heavier. This proportion is about a fourth less than that of his magnitude; so that the same extent of solar substance would be found *four times lighter* than the same extent of terrestrial substance.

THE MOON AND LUNAR PHENOMENA OF OUR SYSTEM.— Next to the greater light that rules the day, the most useful and interesting to us of all the bodies in our universe, is the lesser light that rules the night. The proximity of the moon, the relation in which she is linked to the earth, the power she exerts upon our ocean in drawing up its billows, and the great importance of the lunar theory to safe navigation, have intently fixed the eye of science upon her orb; while the mild radiance with which she shines in the heavens, the advantage of her light to the terrestrial traveller, and the beauty and regularity of her changing phases, have elicited the admiration of barbarian and polished races. The unfailing performance within a definite period of a synodical revolution, or the cycle included between each conjunction with the sun, when she is invisible, called synodical, from the Greek word signifying a coming together, has rendered the moon a convenient time-keeper to men in rude states of society, and won for her the love and respect of savage tribes. Among the wandering hordes of the western continent such a number of moons measures the duration of a journey, and the lapse of events; and successive lunar appearances are discriminated by coincident terrestrial occurrences, as the wild-strawberry moon, the wild rice-gathering moon, the ice-moon, the deer-rutting moon, and the leaf-falling moon. Some of the sacred ceremonies of the Jews, in the early periods of their history, were regulated by the sign of the lunar crescent in the heavens, and the rabbins relate, that persons were stationed on the tops of the mountains to watch for the first appearance of the moon, which event was proclaimed by signal fires throughout the land. For the last six thousand years the eye of man has gazed with delight upon her face, whether in courtly or in rustic life, from old baronial halls or cottages obscure. The meek splendor, the quietude, the fidelity, of which the luminary is a visible image, bewitch the senses, excite the imagination, and have originated some of the most captivating strains of poetic description, among which the Trojan bivouac scene in the Iliad still stands peerless.

> "The troops exulting sat in order round,
> And beaming fires illumin'd all the ground.
> As when the moon, refulgent lamp of night,
> O'er heaven's clear azure spreads her sacred light;
> When not a breath disturbs the deep serene,
> And not a cloud o'ercasts the solemn scene,
> Around her throne the vivid planets roll,
> And stars unnumber'd gild the glowing pole;
> O'er the dark trees a yellower verdure shed,
> And tip with silver every mountain's head;
> Then shine the vales, the rocks in prospect rise,
> A flood of glory bursts from all the skies;
> The conscious swains, rejoicing in the sight,
> Eye the blue vault, and bless the useful light."

An imaginary soliloquy, put into the mouth of Milton by a living writer, strikingly expresses the emotions of such a mind, upon first perceiving the curtains about to fall between him and the resplendence of day and night, through the blindness that attended his declining years. "Beautiful light! beautiful lamp of heaven! what marvel that the blinded and benighted heathen should ignorantly worship thee? What marvel that a thousand altars, in a thousand ages, should have sent up their fumes of adoration unto thee, the mooned Ashtaroth—unto thee, the Ephesian Diana —unto thee, the nightly-visitant of the young-eyed Endymion? What marvel, that to those who knew not, neither had they heard of the One, Uncreate, Invisible, Eternal, thou shouldst have seemed meet Deity to whom to bend the knee, thou first born offspring of his first created gift! thou blessed emanation from his own ethereal glory! What wonder, when I, his humble follower, his ardent though unworthy worshipper—when I, an honest though an erring

Christian, do strive in vain to wean my heart from love of
thee; indoctrinating my spirit, that I may kiss the rod,
with which I am assured, too well, He soon will chasten me,
in changing the fair light, that glorious essence in which my
soul rejoiceth, for one black, everlasting, self-imparted midnight? Yet so it shall be. A few more revolutions of
these puissant planets, a few more mutations of the sweet
returning seasons, and to me there shall be no change again
on earth for ever' no choice between the fairest and the
foulest! no difference of night or day! no charm in the
rich gorgeousness of flowery summer, above the sere and
mournful autumn! no cheery aspect in the piled hearth of
winter' no sweet communion with the human eye compas-
sionate; no intercourse with the great intellect of old—
dead, but surviving still in their sublime and solid pages!"

Our moon is situated in external space, at a mean distance of 237 *thousand miles* from the earth. Great as this
interval is, when compared with the terrestrial extent, it is
only about $\frac{1}{400}$th part the earth's distance from our sun,
and little more than one fourth the diameter of the solar
body. It is owing to this proximity to us, that she occupies so large a space in the heavens, for the lunar diameter
is only 2160 miles. Our own globe is equal in magnitude
to *forty-nine* such bodies, and the sun to near *seventy millions*. If loosened from the action of other forces, the earth
and the moon would fall together by the power of mutual
attraction; but the earth being not only the larger body,
but most dense, and its attraction being far the most powerful, the moon would descend to it, passing the intervening
space in less than five days, our own planet courteously advancing about the distance of its semidiameter to meet the
Satellite.

To the inhabitants of New-York or Boston, whose streets
are splendidly illuminated at night, the presence of the moon
is more a matter of ornament than of use. But it is other-

wise when the day has closed with the mariner at sea; the peasant homeward tracking his way through the drifted snow, the traveler in a strange country; and the barbarous migratory hordes of men. To such, when the day has departed, the moon pursues her nightly circuit through the heavens in beauty and brightness, as a friend in need, chasing away the gloom, revealing the features of the scenery, and disclosing the right path.*

THE STARS OF OUR SYSTEM, AND OF OTHER SYSTEMS,—THEIR NUMBER, DISTANCES, AND MAGNITUDE.—"From the earliest ages," says Professor Mitchell, "these bright and beautiful orbs, which fill the heavens, have fixed the attention—fastened the gaze—excited the curiosity of every contemplative mind. From the Chaldean shepherd, who, while he watched his flocks by night, was wrapped in the contemplation of these bright clusters that rose and silently pursued their solemn course through Heaven, and quietly sank beneath the horizon,—from that early day, through all ages, down to the modern Astronomer, who, with his mighty instruments, penetrates to the utmost bounds of creation, these objects have ever been regarded with peculiar interest and delight."—*New York Tribune.*

The prevailing ideas of men concerning the multitude of the stars, though founded upon wrong premises, are yet in harmony with the literal fact, for the conclusion drawn from the hasty observation of the eye, which a persevering survey would at once disprove, is itself established by telescopic examination. So enormous is the number of the stars, yet so completely incalculable are they, as to admit of their

---

* The comparative proportion which the light of the moon leaves to that of the sun is a problem to the solution of which the attention of several philosophers has been directed. The whole heavens covered with full moons would scarcely make daylight. From various experiments that have been made, it is supposed that the lunar light is only equal to the 300,000th part that of the sun.

being joined with the sand upon the sea-shore, as a figure
of speech denoting ·a. numeration which we cannot de-
:fine. , The common phrase of the Sacred Volume, the hosts
of heaven, alludes 'to their multitude; and the fact is advanced as an illustration of the infinite grasp of the Crea--
tor's mind, that he is acquainted minutely with these multi-
tudinous worlds, which immeasurably exceed our utmost es-
timates. " He calleth them all by names by the greatness
of his might, for that he is strong in power; not one
faileth."

. "There is," says Professor Mitchell, in one of his interesting lectures, " no limit to the stars. Do they go on, the
one behind the other, without end? I answer, no. Then
do you mean to say there is a limit to creation? I answer,
no. I mean to say that the stars are grouped together in
mighty clusters of millions and millions, *as distant from
our clusters as is our sun from their suns.* Herschel it
was that solved this problem. He commences his investiga-
tions by examining the most brilliant part of the Milky Way.
He takes a telescope and finds that this spot yields to him
one hundred beautiful stars, in the distance appearing the
size of hazle-nuts. He takes a greater Telescope—four new
stars are brought up and the others grow brighter and more
beautiful. He takes his forty feet telescope, and he sees all
clear, the stars shining like bright diamonds, and in the
*shade beyond, all is blank. This at once settles the ques-
tion. There are no more stars beyond that limit, and, no
matter how great the depths, he has overcome them all. *But
do we stop here? I answer, no. When we have reached the
utmost limits of our own mighty clusters, then it is that
we begin an investigation of a far different kind. We
pass , the .confines of our own Universe. and. sweep on
through space, millions upon millions of .miles, till, look-
·ing behind, we see the stars that compose our own system,
lying in one vast cluster ; but before, all is blank. Is there*

*nothing there hid in the dark, unfathomable realms?
There are some dim hazy spots looming up in the distance. Bring to our aid the telescope—Lo! there burst
into view tens of thousands suns and stars! Here is
another Universe burst in upon us, and there is not only
one; they are scattered by hundreds and thousands
through space.* Let any one look out at night and count
the stars. You can do it. It has been done. And no eye
has ever been able to count above the horizon, at one time,
over fifteen hundred stars. How close do they appear to
be, one to another, and how numerous their hosts. *Yet
there are more of these mighty Universes scattered through
space than there are stars in our system.* There is one
in the constellation Hercules, which examined with a telescope of low power, presents the appearance of a milky
spot, but with the mighty instrument we use, it is discovered to contain one thousand stars, occupying so small a
point in space that it would seem you might almost grasp
them in your hand. Yet they are so far separated, that
light, which travels twelve millions of miles in a minute,
requires ten thousand years to cross the diameter of its
orbit.* These facts are startling; yet we must receive them,
for the evidence is so strong that it becomes perfectly irresistible."—New York Tribune.*

However marvellous the statement, it is strictly true, that
when we gaze upon the heavens, observe the stars, and note
down their positions, we are witnessing and chronicling
their appearances in by-gone time, and not the present aspect
of the phenomena. The ray that meets the eye from the
nearest siderial object brings intelligence of *its past estate;*
and that Past includes years in relation to the front ranks of
the stellar army, and ages with respect to the general body.

---

* "I fearlessly assert," says Professor Mitchell, "that the day will
never come when the centre of the entire Universe will be found by man."

When we reflect upon these facts, *and remember that the faint nebulous clusters are far more remote from the distinct stars than they from us* — that the light which manifests their presence now may have left its source when the Tudor, Norman, or Saxon race occupied the throne of England — we catch a glimpse of the immensity of space, and of the infinity of that being who originated the great government of which it is the scene.

We have nothing to guide us respecting the magnitude of the stars beyond their visibility, when so vastly remote.— The planet Saturn is magnified by the telescope larger than the moon to the naked eye, *though* 900 *millions of miles distant ;* but instrumental power fails in giving an appreciable magnitude to the stars. It brings countless multitudes into view hid from the unassisted sight; it makes us sensible of their presence; it increases their brilliancy: but beyond this, it supplies us with no information respecting their volume and mass. Halley remarked, that " the diameters of Spica Virginis and Aldebaran are so small, that when they happen to immerge behind the dark edge of the moon, they are so far from losing their light gradually, as they must do if they were of any sensible magnitude, that they vanish at once with all their lustre, and emerge likewise in a moment, not small at first, but at once appear with their full light, even although the emersion happen when very near the cusp, where, if they were ' four seconds in diameter,' they would be many seconds of time in getting entirely separated from the limb. But the contrary appears to all those who have observed the occultations of those bright stars." The largest and most brilliant of the stars, if occulted at the dark limb of the moon, Sir John Herschel observes, " is, as it were, extinguished in mid-air, without notice or visible cause for its disappearance, which, as it happens instantaneously, and without the slightest previous diminution of its light, is always surprising; and if the star

be a large and bright one, even startling from its suddenness." The simple fact of the visibility of the stars across
the mighty expanse which we know to exist between them
and ourselves, necessarily gives us high ideas of their dimensions. Calculations have been made, from a comparison of the light of the stars with that of the sun, but the
result can only be regarded as a rude approximation. Let
us consider the case of Sirius, the brightest in the heavens.
The light of Sirius, as determined by Sir John Herschel,
is 324 *times that of an average star of the sixth magnitude.* The ratio of his light to that of the sun has been
calculated by Dr. Wollaston to be as 1 to 20,000,000,000.
To diminish the light afforded to us by the sun to that; of
Sirius, the sun must be removed to 141,400 times his present distance, or to a distance of 13,433,000,000 miles. *But
no star can be within the range of* 19 *billions of miles.*
The fact therefore of Sirius being immensely larger than
our sun, from the preceding comparison, is at least certain,
though to what extent we know not. Dr. Wollaston as-
sumes, upon reasonable grounds, a much lower limit of possible parallax than that which would give Sirius a computed
distance of 19 billions of miles; and hence concludes, that,
occupying the sun's place, he would appear 3·7 times larger,
and give 13·8 times more light, *or be equal to nearly fourteen suns.*

Eudoxus of Cnidus, a contemporary of Plato, about 370
years before Christ, sent forth a description of the face of
the heavens, containing the names and characters of all the
constellations recognized in his time. Though this production has perished, yet a poetical paraphrase of it, written
about a century later, is still extant, the work of Aratus, a
Cilician, and probably a native of Tarsus. This astronomical poem opens with a statement of the dependence of all
things upon Jupiter, whose children all men are, and who
has given the stars as the guides of agriculture.

"With Jove we must begin; not from Him rove;
Him always praise, for all is full of Jove!
He fills all places where mankind resort,
The wide-spread sea, with ev'ry shelt'ring port.
Jove's presence fills all space, upholds this ball;
All need his aid, his power sustains us all.
For we his offspring are; and He in love
Points out to man his labor from above;
Where signs unerring show when best the soil
By well-tim'd culture shall repay our toil."

NOTE.—The superficial extent of the earth includes upward of a hundred and ninety-seven millions of square miles, and its solid contents amount to two hundred and sixty thousand millions of cubical miles. Huge as this ball is, it sinks into insignificance, when contrasted with Jupiter, Saturn, or Uranus. The areas, and solid contents, of these planets, are about as follows:

	Area.	Solid contents.
Jupiter	24,834,000,000 square miles	368,283,200,000,000 cubic miles
Saturn*	19,600,000,000	261,320,800,000,000
Uranus	3,848,460,000	22,437,804,000,000

Including the other planets and the satellites, their combined surface cannot be estimated at less than sixty thousand millions of square miles, which is about three hundred times the surface of the globe. The mind can only imperfectly embrace this vastness of territory; yet it is but as a province to an empire when compared with a single object in the system—the Sun. In its solid bulk, as already stated, the solar globe is equal to five hundred times the volumes of the planets, and to nearly one and a quarter millions such worlds as ours.

---

* MARS, the nearest to us of the exterior planets, was, in former ages of superstition, the dread of the terrestrials on account of his fiery aspect, and ministered more than any other celestial object to give employment to the astrologers, and to fill their coffers:

"But most is Mars amisse of all the rest;
And next to him old Saturne."

BODIES, AND SUBSTANCES, THAT HAVE FALLEN FROM HEAVEN.—From every region of the globe, and in all ages of time within the range of history, exhibitions of apparent instability in the heavens have been observed, when the curtains of the evening have been drawn. Suddenly, a line of light arrests the eye, darting like an arrow through a varying extent of space, and in a moment the firmament is as sombre as before. The appearance is exactly that of a star falling from its sphere, and hence the popular title of shooting star applied to it. The apparent magnitudes of these meteorites are widely different, and also their brilliancy. Occasionally, they are far more resplendent than the brightest of the planets, and throw a very perceptible illumination upon the path of the observer. A second or two commonly suffices for the individual display, but in some instances it has lasted several minutes. In every climate it is witnessed, and at all times of the year, but most frequently in the autumnal months. As far back as records go, we meet with allusions to these swift and evanescent luminous travelers. Minerva's hasty flight from the peaks of Olympus to break the truce between the Greeks and Trojans, is compared by Homer to the emisssion of a brilliant star. Virgil, in the first book of the Georgics, mentions the shooting stars as prognosticating weather changes:

> " And oft, before tempestuous winds arise,
> The seeming stars fall headlong from the skies,
> And, shooting through the darkness, gild the night
> With sweeping glories and long trains of light."

Antiquity refers us to several objects as having descended from the skies, the gifts of the immortal gods. Such was the Palladium of Troy, the image of the goddess of Ephesus, and the sacred shield of Numa. The folly of the ancients, in believing such narrations has often been the subject of remark; but, however fabulous the particular cases referred *to; the modern have been compelled to renounce their scepticisms respecting the fact itself, of the actual transition of bodies and substances from celestial space to terrestrial regions;* and no doubt the ancient faith upon this subject was founded upon observed events. The following table exhibits a collection of instances of the fall of stones, &c.,

SUBSTANCE.	PLACE.	PERIOD.	AUTHORITY.
Shower of stones	At Rome	Under Tullus Hostilius	Livy.
Shower of stones	At Rome	Consul C. Martius and M. Torquatus.	J. Obsequens.
Shower of iron	In Laconia	Year before the defeat of Crassus	Pliny.
Shower of mercury	In Italy		Dion.
Large stone	Near the river Negos, Thrace	Second year of the 78th Olmpiad	Pliny.
Three large stones	In Thrace	Year before J.C. 452	Ch. of Count Marcellin.
Shower of fire	At Quesnoy	January 4, 1717	Geoffroy le Cadet.
Stone of 72 lbs.	Near Larissa, Macedonia	January, 1706	Paul Lucas.
About 1200 stones—one of 120 lbs.	Near Padua, in Italy	In 1510	Garden, Varcit.
Another of 60 lbs.	On Mount Vaiser, Provence	November 27, 1627.	Gassendi.
Shower of sand for 15 hours	In the Atlantic	April 6, 1719	Pere le Feuillee.
Shower of fire and sulphur	Sodom and Gomorra		Moses.
Sulphurous rain	In the Duchy of Mansfield	In 1658	Spangenburgh.
The same	Copenhagen	In 1646	Olaus Wormius.
Shower of sulphur	Brunswick	October, 1721	Siegesbaar.
Shower of unknown matter	Ireland	In 1695	Muschenbrock.
Two large stones, weighing 20 lbs.	Liponas, in Bresse	September, 1753	Lalande.
A stony mass	Niort, Normandy	In 1750	Lalande.
A stone of 7¼ lbs.	At Luce, in Le Maine	In 1768	Bachelay.
A stone	At Aire, in Artois	In 1768	Gurssonde de Boyaval.
Extensive shower of stones	In Le Cotentin		Morand
About twelve stones	Environs of Agen	July 24, 1790	St. Amand, Baudin, &c.
A large stone of 56 lbs.	Sienna, Tuscany	July, 1794	Earl of Bristol.
A stone of about 30 lbs.	Wold Cottage, Yorkshire	December 13, 1795	Captain Topham.
A stone of about 10 lbs.	Sale, Department of the Rhone	March 17, 1798	Lelievre and De Dree
Shower of stones	In Portugal	February 19, 1796	Southey.
Shower of stones	Benares, East Indies	December 19, 1798	J. Lloyd Williams, Esq.
Shower of stones	At Plann, near Tabor, Bohemia	July 3, 1763	B. De Born.
Mass of iron, 70 cubic feet	America	April 5, 1800	Philosophical Mag.
Mass of iron, 14 quintals	Abakauk, Siberia	Very old	Pallas, Chladni, &c.
Shower of stones	Barboutan, near Roquefort	July, 1789	Darcet, Jun., Lomet, &c.
Large stone of 260 lbs.	Ensisheim, Upper Rhine	November 7, 1492	Butenschoen.
Two stones, 200 and 300 lbs	Near Verona	In 1762	Acad. de Board.
A stone of 20 lbs.	Sules, near Ville Franche	March 12, 1798	De Dree.
Several stones from 10 to 17 lbs.	Near L'Aigle, Normandy.	April 26, 1803	Fourcroy

together with the eras of their descent, and the persons on whose evidence the facts rest; but the list might be greatly extended.

The following are the principal facts with reference to these substances, upon which general dependence may be placed. Immediately after the descent of the stones or other bodies, they are intensely hot. They are covered with a fused black incrustation consisting chiefly of oxide of iron, and what is most remarkable, their chemical analysis develops the same substances in nearly the same proportions, though one may have reached the earth in India and another in England. Their specific gravities are about the same; considering 1000 as the proportionate number for the specific gravity of water, that of some of the stones has been found to be—

Ennesheim stone -	3233	Yorkshire	- -	3508
Benares - - -	3352	Bachalay's	- -	3535
Sienna - - -	3418	Bohemia -	- -	4281
Gassendi's - - -	3456			

The greater specific gravity of the Bohemian stone arose from its containing a larger proportion of iron. An analysis of one of the stones that fell at L'Aigle gives—

Silica - -	46 per cent	Nickel - - -	-	2
Magnesia -	10	Sulphur - -	-	5
Iron - -	45	Zinc - - -	-	1

Iron is found in all these bodies, and in a considerable quantity, with the rare metal nickel. It is a singular fact, *that though a chemical examination of their composition has not discovered any substance with which we were not previously acquainted, yet no other bodies have yet been found, native to the earth, which contain the same ingredients combined. Neither products of the volcanoes, whether extinct or in action, nor the stratified or unstratified rocks, have exhibited a sample of that combination of metallic and earthy substances which the meteoric stones present.* During the era that science has admitted their path to the earth as a physical truth, scarcely amounting to half a century, few years have elapsed without a known instance of descent occurring in some region of the globe. To the list, already given, upward of seventy cases might be added, which have transpired during the last forty years. A report relating to one of the most recent, which fell in a valley near the Cape of Good Hope, with the affidavits of the witnesses, was communicated to the Royal Society by Sir John Herschel, in March 1840. Previously to the descent, the usual sound of explosion was heard, and some of the fragments falling upon grass caused it instantly to smoke, and were too hot to admit of being touched. When, however, we consider the wide range of the ocean, and the vast unoccupied regions of the globe, its mountains, deserts, and forests, we can hardly fail to admit that the observed cases of descent must form but a small proportion of the actual number ; and obviously in countries upon which the human race are thickly planted, many may escape notice through descending in the night, and will lie imbedded in the soil till some accidental circumstance exposes their existence. Some too are no doubt completely fused and dissipated in the atmosphere, while others move by us horizontally as brilliant lights, and pass into the depths of space. The volume of some of these passing bodies is very great. *One which traveled within twenty-five miles of the surface, and cast down a fragment, was supposed to weigh upward of half a million of tons.* But for its great velocity of about twenty miles in a second, the whole mass would have been precipited to the earth.

A multitude of theories have been devised to account for the origin of these remarkable bodies, but hitherto no definite conclusion has been arrived at respecting them. Admitting the existence of such bodies to be placed beyond all doubt, the question of their origin, whether original accumulations of matter, old as the planetary orbs, or the dispersed trains of comets, *or the remains of a ruined world*, is a point beyond the power of the human understanding to reach.

COMETS.—Of all the celestial objects which have arrested the attention of mankind, none have excited such general and lively apprehension as that of comets. A volume of no inconsiderable dimensions might be compiled, and not without interest, from the accounts of old chronicles respecting their appearances, registering the quaintly expressed opinions of the chroniclers concerning them, the terrestrial events they have tacked to them as effects to a cause, and the deportment to which men have been moved by the apparition of

> " the blazing star
> Threat'ning the world with famine, plague, and war;
> To princes, death; to kingdoms, many crosses;
> To all estates, inevitable losses;
> To herdsmen, rot; to ploughmen, hapless seasons,
> To sailors, storms; to cities, civil treasons."

We have the word comet from the Greek χόμη, or hair, a title which had its origin in the hairy appearance often exhibited, a nebulosity, haze, or kind of luminous vapor, being one of the characteristics of these bodies. Their general features are a definite point or nucleus, a nebulous light surrounding the nucleus, the hair, called by the French *chevelure*, and a luminous train preceding or following the nucleus. Milton refers to one of these attributes in a passage which countenances the popular superstition :

> " Satan stood
> Unterrified, and like a comet burned,
> That fires the length of Ophiucus huge,
> In th' arctic sky, and from its horrid hair,
> Shakes, pestilence and war."

Anciently, when the train preceded the nucleus, as is the case when a comet has passed its perihelion, and recedes

from the sun, it was called the beard, being only termed the
tail when seen following the nucleus as the sun is approached. This distinction has disappeared from all modern
astronomical works, and the latter name is given to the ap-
pendage, whatever its apparent position. Neither this
luminous attendant, the tail, nor the nucleus, are now considered essential-cometary elements, but all bodies are
classed as comets which have a motion of their own, and
describe orbits of an extremely elongated form. There
are several plain points of difference between comets and
planets. The planets move in the same direction from
west to east, which is astronomically called direct motion;
but the movements of comets are often from east to west, or
retrograde. The orbits of all the planets are confined to a
zone of no great breadth on either side of the ecliptic; but
the paths of comets cut the ecliptic in every direction, some
being even perpendicular to it, traversing the heavens in all
parts. The contrast is striking likewise between the forms
of their respective orbits. A hoop will with no great inac-
curacy represent the courses of the planets, but the cometary
paths are immensely elongated ellipses, their breadth bearing no proportion to their length. Only one end of the
ellipse lies within the visible limits of the solar system, in
the case of the great majority of these bodies. They only
visit our gaze therefore during one part of their course, and
that a very small part, traveling during the rest of their
journey far beyond the range of the most distant planet,
into spaces inaccessible to our sight. The circumstances of
their motions plainly distinguish them from the planets,
fixed stars, and nebulæ. Planetary configuration is also
uniformly globular, but the external appearances of comets
exhibit great diversities of form, from that of an irregular
wisp of cloud to a simple spherical luminosity, or a strongly
defined scimitar-shaped aspect.

" A pathless comet, and a curse,
The menace of the universe ;
Still rolling on with innate force,
Without a sphere, without a course."

We believe it is generally understood that Halley was the
first to foretel the precise periodical return of one of these
bodies. This, however, has been disputed, and assigned to
Newton, on evidence recently detailed in one of the leading
journals, but which certainly cannot be admitted to invali-
date his pretensions. It is affirmed that previously to the
appearance of the comet of 1736, Colonel Guise told Whiston that Sir Isaac Newton had said in his presence, that
" though he would not say he was sure of it, nor would
publish it, he had some reason to believe that a comet would
return about the latter end of 1736." Another witness
also, Mr. Howard, is cited, as having heard him make a
similar remark ; and upon being questioned concerning it,
it is stated that " he seemed to draw back, as sorry that he
had said so much, but still could not deny that he had such
an expectation." Whiston therefore says :—" As far as we
yet know, Sir Isaac is the very first man, and this the very
first instance, where the coming of a comet has been predict-
ed beforehand, and has actually come according to that prediction, from the beginning of the creation to this day."
Thompson seems to fall in with this idea in panegyrising the
great philosopher :—

" He, first of men, with awful wing pursued
The comet through the long elliptic curve,
As 'long innumerous worlds he wound his way,
Till to the forehead of our evening sky
Return'd, the blazing wonder glares anew,
And o'er the trembling nations shakes dismay "

This is all the evidence that can be arrayed in favor of
Newton ; and obviously its hearsay source, with the dubious
tone of the testimony reported, cannot weigh a feather in

the scale against the claims of Halley, whose prediction was the result of careful comparison, and as such boldly published to the world.

In the autumn of 1811, within the memory of many of the present generation, by far the finest comet suddenly appeared to adorn our heavens, that has been seen since the age of Newton. It was first beheld in Great Britain in the beginning of September, and was visible for more than three months in succession to the naked eye, shining with great splendor, the observed of all observers. This was a comet of the first class in point of magnitude and luminosity. Its brilliant tail, at its greatest elongation, *had an extent of* 123 *millions of miles, by a breadth of* 15 *millions ;* and thus supposing the nucleus of the comet to have been placed on the sun, and the tail in the plane of the orbits of the planet it would have reached over those of Mercury, Venus, the Earth, and have bordered on that of Mars. At its nearest approach to us, the comet was yet distant 141 millions of miles, so that even had the tail pointed to the earth, its extremity would have been 18 millions of miles away from its surface. The following are the calculations respecting its period of revolution:

Years.			Authority.	Years.				Authority.
3056	-	-	Callendrelli	3757	-	-	-	Ferrer
3383	-	-	- Bessel	4237	-		-	Lemaur.

The mind is astounded at a journey requiring the least of these cycles for its accomplishment — a period equal to that extending from the fabulous age of Grecian story to the present; nor is the thought less wonderful, of the chain of solar influence following the traveler through the whole of its course, and preventing its elopement into the regions of immensity. The laws of the system, indeed, impose upon the long-period comets vast differences of velocity. The same body that rushes round the sun at the nearest point of contact with prodigious speed, will move but sluggishly through the remoter parts of its orbit. In computing the periodic time of the comet of 1811, Lemaur assigned 775 years to the half of the ellipse nearest the sun, and 3462 to the more distant half. The appearance of this comet was strikingly ornamental to the evening sky. Many a reaper late in the harvest field stayed his hand, and many a peasant homeward-bound stopped in the way, to gaze upon the celestial novelty as it grew into distinctness with the declining day. The Ettrick shepherd has left a memorial of his impressions in the well-known lines:

> "Stranger of heaven, I bid thee hail!
> Shred from the pall of glory riven,
> That flashest in celestial gale—
> Broad pennon of the King of Heaven

> "Whate'er portends thy front of fire,
> And streaming locks so lovely pale;
> Or peace to man, or judgments dire,
> Stranger of heaven, I bid thee hail!"

NEBULÆ.—Far more astonishing than any of the details upon which we have hitherto dwelt, are those relating to the class of celestial objects we have now to consider, the investigation of which is at present the highest branch of practical astronomy. In directing our attention to Nebulæ, we leave what may comparatively be called *home regions*, strange as the phrase appears, when we recollect the distance intervening between us and the nearest of the stars. But such language is strictly appropriate with reference to the stars visible to the naked eye, and reached by ordinary telescopic aid. They form our firmament or cluster, near the centre of which the solar system is supposed to be situate, the Milky Way being apparently its outward boundary. Yet besides this province with which we are connected, incalculably vast as it is, perfectly inestimable both in length, breadth, depth, and height, *there are other provinces within view, equally as capacious, distinct firmaments of clusters, scattered through those territories of the universe that are accessible to our gaze; and could we be removed to any of them, the whole of that great scheme of existence circumscribed by the Milky Way, might seem compressed into a small globular patch in space, the aspect presented by the nebulæ to ourselves.* The term nebula, signifying a cloud or mist, is a denomination given to spots of pale light, which are sprinkled in the heavens, a few of which may be detected by the unaided eye. They vary considerably in shape, size, and luminosity; and occur in numbers, which every improvement of the telescope increases.

It was one of the great tasks of Sir William Herschel to gauge the heavens, and to ascertain the relative distances of the resolved and resolvable clusters; and, as many of those views which were deemed wild and visionary by his compeers, have, since his day, been triumphantly established, his inquiries and conclusions in general are entitled to attention and confidence. To the centres of the easily resolved spherical nebulæ of the largest diameter, he assigned a remoteness 400 times that of Sirius. Those of half their diameter, whose stars appear to be more closely wedged, he supposed to be double the distance of the former; and at four times their distance, or 2400 times more remote than Sirius, he placed those clusters which plainly indicate resolvability, but whose components are not with our present means apprehensible. In the last case we have an extent of space equal to at least 45,000,000,000,000,000, or forty-five thousand billions of miles. The dumb-bell nebula is certainly not within that range, and probably much farther off. Light, which comes to us from the sun in eight minutes—flashing along at the immense rate of, 190,000 miles in a second of time, or nearly twelve millions of miles in a minute, *would require upwards of seven thousand years to perform its passage across the gulf!* But Herschel went to a still more tremendous depth in space—that of 35,175 times the distance of Sirius — as the site of some clusters; — a comparison with which the distance of the stars themselves from us, mighty as it appears, shrinks into insignificance. Such is Creation! or at least that part of it with which we have some acquaintance. These are views which render the language of Coleridge not chargeable with extravagance: *"It is surely not impossible,"* said that highly gifted man, *" that to some infinitely superior Being the whole universe may be as one plain — the distance between planet and planet being only as the pores in a grain of sand, and the spaces between system and system no greater than the intervals between one grain and a grain adjacent !"*

The dimensions of one of these nebula alone is so enormous, that it subtends an angle of nearly 10′, and supposing it at the distance of a star of the eighth magnitude, its size must be at least 3,208,600,000,000,000,000, or more than three trillions of times that of our sun. Upon comparing the present appearance of this great nebula with former drawings of it, it appears to have undergone some marked changes, at least if the older representations are to be depended upon. The following memorandum was made by Herschel when he viewed it in 1774: "Its shape is not like that which Dr. Smith has delineated in his 'Optics,' though somewhat resembling it; from this we may infer that there are undoubtedly changes among the regions of the fixed stars; and perhaps, from a careful observation of this lucid spot, something may be concluded concerning the nature of it." What this immense looming mass portends, we know not, *but the surmise is not improbable, that here we have the germ of systems of worlds to be evolved in future ages, where Life, Beauty, and Intelligence are destined to play their various phases.*

An object of the same *class* appears in the girdle of Andromeda, called the " transcendently beautiful Queen of the nebulæ," the oldest known nebula, supposed also to be one of the nearest. It is visible to the naked eye in the absence of the moon, and has often been mistaken for a comet. A notice of it occurs as early as the commencement of the tenth century. The first telescopic view was obtained by Simon Marius, December 15, 1612, who compared it to a candle shining through a horn, that is, a diluted light increasing in density towards a centre. This nebula is of an oval or lenticular shape, and forms nearly a right-angled triangle with Almaach Mirach, the two chief stars of Andromeda. A good eye may pick it up on a favorable night, by projecting a line from Sheratan, the second star in Aries, through Mirach to about 44° beyond. It is about half a degree long, and from 15' to 20' broad. Herschel, who deemed this one of the nearest nebulæ in the heavens, remarks: "The brightest part of it approaches to the resolvable nebulosity, and begins to show a faint red color; which from many observations on the magnitude and color of nebulæ, I believe to be an indication that its distance in the colored part does not exceed 2000 times the distance of Sirius." This is the rather extensive interval of 38,000,000,000,000,000, of miles, *a space which light will require more than* 6000 *years to traverse, so that a ray that now meets the eye must have started from its source before the creation of man, and a ray that is now leaving it will not accomplish the distance till the world is six thousand years older.*

Those who have treated the nebulæ hypothesis with ridicule have strangely forgotten what is daily passing before their eyes—forgotten the uniform plan of Providence with reference to the world in which we live. What is man—full-grown, active, intellectual man—as he appears in the maturity of his powers, the noontide of his day, but an example of ascension from a crude to a higher condition? By gradual and slow degrees, he acquires his vigor of frame, fluency of speech, agility of movement, and furniture of mind.

We have no more occasion to stumble at the idea that

our world dates its origin *from a few primordial elements,
endowed with properties to complete the structure,* than a
colony of ants, at a tree root, would have cause to start at
the fact, could they be made cognizant of it, that leaves,
branches, and trunk proceeded from a single seed. The law
that unites the atoms that compose the earth, forms every
rain-drop, and moulds the tear that trickles down the cheek
of sorrow—in prevailing operation millions of leagues away
from our terrestrial residence, binding together in spherical
masses whole sidereal systems. Such a fact, however, commonly suggests no farther remarks than that the laws of
nature every where prevail, and with this, thought in general
ends. But "*what,*" says Paley, "*do we mean by the laws
of nature, or by any law? Effects are produced by
power, and not by laws. A law cannot execute itself. A
law refers us to an agent.*" An irresistible conviction is
forced upon us, of the universal agency, and, consequently,
the omnipresence of one Lawgiver, by the universal presence and execution of kindred laws; and confessedly incom-
prehensible as is the *modus* of His operation, it would be
not more irreligious to stumble at this than unphilosophical,
considering the immense amount of things of which we
have certain evidence that they are, without having any
glimpse as to how they are. We cannot at all understand the
physical agency of the Deity; but paying deference to the
strong facts of nature, we are led to the conclusion that He

"Lives through all life, extends through all extent
Spreads undivided, operates unspent."

However it may savor of the gigantesque, it is suffi-
ciently evidenced *that an area of the heavens not exceeding
$\frac{1}{10}$ of the lunar diameter, contains a system of stars ri-
valling in number those which constitute our firmament,
and appearing only as a single faint luminosity to us
Yet there are thousands of areas so occupied.* It follows,

therofore, that our firmament is but one of a series: one of
the smaller chambers in the great mansion of the universe.
All the stars and constellations that shine in the midnight
sky, constitute a stellar scheme which is but a unit of a
countless number. As seen from the faint objects we discern in the side of Hercules and the sword-handle of Per-
seus, our whole sphere would be compressed into a small
streak of light, and appear in space like a snow flake in our
atmosphere !

" Distrusting the power of the Refracting Telescope,"
says Professor Mitchell, " Lord Rosse determined to give
his energies to the construction of a Reflecting Telescope,
that would enable him to make grander discoveries than had
hitherto been made   He wanted an instrument that would
burst through the barriers that had hitherto bounded human
vision ; that would show him what lay in the vast deep
beyond. I need not detail to you the construction of this
mighty instrument. Instead of limiting it to four feet
in diameter, as Herschel did, he has given his speculum six
feet, with a focal distance of sixty feet. The power of this
instrument is almost incredible. Such is its capacity *that
if a star of the first magnitude were removed to such a
distance that its light would be sixty thousand years in
traveling to the earth, this telescope would reveal it ; were
it removed so far that its light would be three millions of
years in reaching us, this telescope would show it to the
human eye.* With such an instrument, then it is not wonderful that great discoveries should be made. It has but
been pointed to the heavens ; we have only entered upon the
beginning of its career, but it has already accomplished
mighty things. There are scattered throughout the heavens objects nebulous in their appearance which would not
yield up their character to the instruments heretofore employed ; but this instrument resolves them completely.
Among the different objects that have been subjected to its

scrutiny, is the wonderful nebula in the constellation Orion.
I have had an opportunity of examining it. It is one of the
most curious objects in the whole heavens. It is not round,
and it throws off furious lights. This object has been subjected to the examination of every instrument from the time
of Herschel, but it grew more and more mysterious, more
difficult to understand, more strange and diverse in its character. When Lord Ross's great telescope was directed to
its examination, it for a long time resisted its power. He
found it necessary to wait night after night and month
after month, until finally a favoring combination of circumstances gave to him a pure atmosphere. He directed his
telescope to the object, and lo! its station revealed itself, the
stars of which it is composed burst upon the sight for the
first time, and the problem was solved forever. Here is one
of the mightiest triumphs of this instrument, but it has
gone on from point to point revealing combinations of stars
wonderful beyond what the imagination could conceive. "—
New York Tribune.

MEMOIR OF GALILEO.

" When in dungeon damply lying,
Faint and tortured, hardly dying,
Yet for truth, with honest pride,
Yet, ' It moves! it moves !" he cried "

GALILEO GALILEI, the eldest son of Vincentio Galilei,
was born at Pisa in Italy, on the 15th of February, 1564.
Like most experimental philosophers, Galileo, in his earliest
years, gave indications of that bent of mind, and intellectual superiority, which has made him rank so high among
the philosophers of antiquity. Although his father was by
no means wealthy, Galileo received a tolerable education.
He was desirous of following the profession of a painter ;
but in obedience to his father's desire, he entered as a scholar
of arts at the university of Pisa, on the 5th of November,
1581, and applied himself to the study of medicine. Music
was a favorite study of Galileo's. In studying the principles of this science, he found it necessary to learn something
of geometry, and commenced with Euclid's Elements. The
demonstrations of the mathematician, and the new and wondrous truths which this science unfolds, took such hold of
the ardent mind of Galileo, that after many fruitless attempts to confine him to the study of medicine, his father
gave up the attempt, and allowed him to follow his own
inclinations. From Euclid he ascended to the higher mathe-
maticians ; and, while studying Archimedes' treatise on hy-

drostatics, he wrote an essay on the hydrostatical balance, explaining its construction, and the mode by which the philosopher of Syracuse detected the fraud committed by the jewellers making Hiero's crown. This work introduced Galileo to Guido Ubaldi, an eminent mathematician, who engaged him to investigate the subject of the centre of gravity in solid bodies; and the treatise which he produced upon this subject was the foundation of his future celebrity

Through his connexion with Ubaldi, Galileo was appointed lecturer on mathematics at Pisa in 1589, with a yearly salary of sixty crowns, which he increased by devoting some time to private teaching. At the early age of eighteen, Galileo doubted the philosophy of Aristotle; and on his establishment at Pisa, commenced to overthrow the doctrines of this philosopher. His first inquiries were into the mechanical doctrines of Aristotle, which he soon discovered to be untenable. The errors which he found existing, he exposed to his pupils, and a rancorous controversy commenced between the followers of Aristotle on the one side, and Galileo and his pupils on the other. Argument, and even experiment, failed in convincing Galileo's opponents. The doctrine of Aristotle, that the heavier of two falling bodies would fall quicker, was proved by the experiment of dropping bodies of different weights from the leaning tower at Pisa; but although these bodies struck the ground nearly at the same instant, the followers of Aristotle remained unconvinced, or at least unconverted. Conscious of his superiority, and the truth of his doctrines, Galileo turned not only the powers of argument, but the shafts of ridicule and sarcasm against his opponents; thus raising up a personal enmity, which afterwards developed itself in bitter persecution. Other circumstances increased the rancor of his enemies, and at last made his position so uncomfortable, that he gave up his situation at Pisa, and accepted the professorship of mathematics at the university of Padua, with an income of 180 florins. The death of his father having burdened Galileo with the family, he had to apply himself here as at Pisa, to private teaching. Notwithstanding his public and private duties, however, he still found leisure to make several discoveries and inventions, which were circulated in manuscript amongst his friends. Some of these abused the confidence reposed in them, and published several of Galileo's inventions as their own.

The doctrines of Copernicus, regarding the stability of the sun and the revolution of the planets, were the subject of disputation among the learned in the time of Galileo. He early became a convert to the new doctrines, and believed in them even at the time he was teaching the opposite or Ptolemaic system, which regarded the earth as stationary, and the sun a revolving body. Shortly after he went to Padua, he published a treatise on the sphere, in which the system of Ptolemy was supported by the very arguments which he afterward ridiculed. It is rather considered, however, that it was some time after the publication of this treatise that Galileo changed his opinions. About this time he commenced a correspondence with Kepler, the German astronomer, which continued till his death.

In 1593, he contracted a chronic disorder, from inadvertently sleeping at an open window, which afflicted him at intervals during the rest of his life. At this time, Galileo's reputation as a philosopher was widely extended all over Europe, and many of the nobility became his pupils. His first engagement as professor at Padua was for six years. On the expiry of this term, he was re-engaged for other six years, at an advanced salary of 320 florins. The first important discovery of Galileo was, that the vibrations of a pendulum are performed in equal times, whatever be the size of the arc described, within certain limits. In 1604, a new star was discovered by astronomers in the constellation of Ophiucus, and formed the subject of much speculation By some it was set down as a meteor; but from the absence of parallax, Galileo proved it to be one of the fixed stars, situated far beyond the bounds of our own system.

Galileo was again appointed professor at Padua, in 1606, and his salary increaséd to 520 florins. So great had his fame as a philosopher arisen, that the lecture-room could not contain his hearers, which obliged him often to lecture in the open air. Among other pursuits, he investigated the properties of the loadstone, and discovered a method of arming them, so as to double their magnetic power. Galileo still kept up communication with the family of the Duke of Tuscany, who had been his early patron. Cosmo, who had succeeded his father Ferdinand, had been one of Galileo's pupils, and being imbued with an ardent wish to promote science, formed the desire of attaching his former master to his household. Negotiations were accordingly commenced. His salary, as professor at Padua, was to be greatly increased on the expiry of his engagement. The seclusion of private life, however, offered far greater charms to the studious philosopher. He was anxious to escape the performance of public and private duties, which continually interrupted his own studies. He accordingly accepted the situation of philosopher and principal mathematician to the Grand Duke of Tuscany, with a salary of 1000 florins, and took up his residence at Florence. The only duties attached to this situation, were, to lecture occasionally to sovereign princes. It was expressly stipulated that he should have the most perfect command of his own time, to devote to study and the completion of some projected works.

During the progress of the arrangements for leaving Padua, Galileo paid a visit to Venice. Here he became informed of an optical instrument, presented by a Dutchman to Prince Maurice of Nassau, which possessed the property of enlarging objects, and bringing them nearer the observer. This was confirmed by a letter which Galileo received a few days afterward from Paris. 'To the consideration of this subject he immediately applied himself, and the first night after his return to Padua, he discovered what he sought in the doctrine of refracting light. He fitted a spectacle-glass to each end of a leaden tube, one of which was plano-convex, and the other plano-concave, and on applying his eye to the concave glass, he found that it magnified. Delighted with his discovery, he carried his little instrument in triumph to Venice, where it created a most intense excitement, and for a month thousands flocked to see it. He made a present of it to the Venetian Senate, and received in return a perpetual grant of the professorship at Padua, and an increase of salary from 520 to 1000 florins. It was shortly after this that he entered the household of the Grand Duke of Tuscany.

After disposing of his first instrument, which magnified only three times, Galileo applied himself to the making of another, which magnified eight times, and "at length," as he says himself, "sparing neither labor nor expense," he constructed an instrument which magnified thirty times. With this instrument he discovered the inequalities in the moon's surface. "The dark and luminous spaces he regarded as indicating seas and continents, which reflected in different degrees the incidental light of the sun; and he ascribed the phosphorescence, as it has been improperly called, or the secondary light which is seen on the dark limb of the moon in her first and last quarters, to the reflection of the sun's light from the earth." With the telescope he discovered a striking difference between the appearance of the fixed stars and the planets. The latter exhibited round and well-defined discs like the moon, while the former, even of the first magnitude, appeared but as lucid points. He was likewise enabled to resolve portions of nebulæ and clusters, which appeared to be hazy spots in the heavens, into distinct and numerous stars.

On the 7th of January, 1610, he discovered three of

Jupiter's satellites. When he first observed them, two were on the east side, and one on the west side of the planet, all in a straight line, parallel to the ecliptic, and much brighter than fixed stars of their magnitude. He regarded them at first as fixed stars; but, on chancing to direct his attention to them again on the 8th of January, he found all the three to be on the west side of Jupiter, and nearer each other. Disregarding the circumstance of these stars having approached each other, he considered how Jupiter could be to the east of them, when the day before he had been to the west of two of them; and the conclusion he came to was, " that the motion of Jupiter was *direct* contrary to the astronomical calculations, and that he had got before these two stars by his own motion." On the 10th, however, another observation showed him only two stars, and both on the *east* side of Jupiter. It was evident that the planet could not have moved from west to east on the 8th of January, and two days after have moved from east to ·west. Under these circumstances he came to the conclusion, that the different appearances arose from the motion of the stars themselves. On the 11th, there were two stars on the east side of Jupiter, but the one was twice the size of the other. " This fact threw a new light upon Galileo's difficulties, and he immediately drew the conclusion which he considered to be indubitable, 'that there were in the heavens *three stars*, which revolved round Jupiter in the same manner as *Venus* and *Mercury* revolve round the sun.' "* On the 13th, Galileo discovered the fourth satellite of Jupiter. Having made these discoveries, he named them the *Medician stars*, in honor of his patron, Cosmo de Medici, grand-duke of Tuscany, and published an account of them in a work entitled the "*Sidereal Messenger.*"

These discoveries, the fruits of the newly discovered tel-

---

* " Martyrs of Science," by Sir D. Brewster.

escope, astonished the whole scientific world. The ideas,
however, which Galileo enunciated in his "Sidereal Messenger," were attacked on all hands by the Aristotelians.
They even denied the existence of the four satellites which
Galileo had discovered: some affirming he was deceived by
reflected rays; and others, that it was a *ruse* to afford himself a subject for discussion. Their existence having been
at last indisputably established, others began to claim the
priority of discovery, and to pretend that they had discovered additional satellites of Jupiter. Some gave this
planet as many as twelve moons; but they were gradually
found out to be fixed stars, and Galileo remained the original discoverer of the four secondary planets.

Before the close of 1610, Galileo discovered Saturn's ring,
although not conscious of its true nature, or the appearance which it presents when highly magnified. He described Saturn as a triple star, each retaining its relative
position. Shortly after, he discovered that Venus presented
phases like the moon, when at different parts of her orbit.
He likewise discovered spots on the sun's surface, from which
he calculated that that luminary had a motion on its axis,
completed in about twenty-eight days. In 1612, he published a treatise on floating bodies, displaying a knowledge
of many true principles in hydrostatics. It was violently
attacked; but the master mind of Galileo refuted his opponents as soon almost as they appeared.

The great objection raised by the priesthood and followers of Aristotle, against the doctrines advanced by Galileo,
was, *that they were contrary to Scripture, and ran coun-
ter to the doctrine of the Church.* In refuting these and
other objections, Galileo added to the calm arguments of
reason the bitterness of sarcasm. In 1613 he published a
letter to prove that the Scriptures were not to be taken as
guides in philosophy, *and that the language found in the
Bible was wrongly interpreted,* and might with equal pro-

priety have been urged against the doctrines of Ptolemy. The storm which had been gathering over the devoted head of the philosopher at last broke forth. He was denounced from the pulpit by one Caccini, a friar. The general of the order to which this friar belonged apologized for this attack; and stimulated by a strong love of truth, and to silence his antagonists, Galileo published another letter *defending his views of Scripture, applied to his own and the system of Ptolemy.*

These letters were denounced to the Inquisition, and steps taken to bring Galileo before the bar of that sanguinary tribunal. It is a disputed point whether Galileo, on hearing of the steps taken against him, went to Rome of his own accord, or whether he was cited there. He appeared at Rome at the latter end of 1615, and was shortly after summoned before the Inquisition, to answer the charges of having heretically maintained the motion of the earth, and the stability of the sun, and with having taught it to others. The Inquisitors met, and after considering these charges, decreed, that Galileo should be enjoined to renounce those opinions, and to pledge himself neither to teach, defend, nor publish them; and that, in the event of refusal, he should be thrown into prison. To these Galileo agreed, and was dismissed.

Philip III, King of Spain, a country at that time extensively engaged in maritime enterprise, had offered a reward for the discovery of an improved mode of finding the longitude at sea. To this problem Galileo turned his attention, and proposed to make the satellites of Jupiter subservient to effecting this purpose. Communications on the subject were made to the Spanish court, and so great was Galileo's desire to carry out his project, that he offered to go to Spain and reside there till he had communicated a knowledge of his method. Nothing satisfactory came out of these negociations, which were occasionally revived during a period of

ten or twelve years. In 1618, three comets visited our system, and engaged the attention of the learned men of the
time. Galileo was prevented by illness, from making observations on these erratic bodies; but he became deeply involved in controversy respecting them, and, it is asserted,
maintained the opinion that they were meteors.

Cardinal Maffeo Barberini, a sincere friend of Galileo's,
was raised to the papal throne; and, although in ill-health
at the time, Galileo set out for Rome, to congratulate the
new pope on his elevation, and secure a continuation of his
friendship. He was kindly received; and after repeated
audiences, the receipt of several presents, and the promise
of a pension to his son, he was dismissed by the pope with
every expression of friendship and regard.

Galileo was scarcely free from the fangs of the inquisition, than his innate love of truth, and abhorrence of a system which set the erring judgment of men superior to the dictates of reason and the phenomena of nature, prompted him
to repeat his offences. In 1618, he communicated to the
archduke Leopold his theory of the tides; and, in doing so,
alluded, in sarcastic terms, to the proceedings of the church.
The same spirit pervaded others of his writings. In 1632,
he published a work, under the title of the *System of the
World of Galileo Galilei*, demonstrating the Copernican
theory. To shield himself from Inquisitorial persecution,
he adopted a system of dialogue, in which three assumed
characters are exhibited in debate upon the respective systems. One of these takes up, and defends the system of
Copernicus; another suggests doubts and difficulties; and
the third stands up for the system of Ptolemy. This work
attracted great notice, and the church having committed
itself by denouncing the new doctrines, at once laid on its
strong arm to crush the audacious innovator of its dogmas.

Proceedings were immediately adopted to summon Galileo
again before the Inquisition. Representations were made

through the Tuscan ambassador at the papal court, to obtain a written statement of the charges, that Galileo might prepare for his defence. This, however, was refused, and a summons was soon issued for him to appear at Rome. At this time a contagious epidemic was raging in Tuscany, and a strict quarantine was enforced at Rome. Representations were made of the miseries which a journey under these circumstances would impose upon Galileo, who at the time was suffering from advanced age and ill health. Personal attendance was however peremptorily demanded. Some respect was certainly paid to the talents and infirmities of Galileo during the progress of his trial. He was allowed to reside in the palace of the Tuscan ambassador, and even permitted to visit the public gardens

On the 22d of June, 1633, the Inquisitors assembled to pronounce sentence on the philosopher. From passages in the sentence, it is suspected that Galileo was put to the torture. The sentence itself is too long for insertion; but the following extract will convey an idea of its nature:—

"By the desire of his Holiness, and of the most eminent Lords Cardinals of this supreme and universal Inquisition, the two propositions of the stability of the sun and the motion of the earth were *qualified* by the theological qualifiers as follows :

1st "The proposition that the sun is the centre of the world, and immoveable from its place, is absurd, philosophically false, and formally *heretical*; because it is expressly contrary to Holy Scripture.

2d "The proposition that the earth is not the centre of the world, nor immoveable; but that it moves and also with a diurnal motion, is absurd, philosophically false; and theologically considered, at least *erroneous* in faith.

* * * * * * * * *

"We decree that the book of the Dialogues of Galileo Galilei be prohibited by edict; we condemn you to the prison of this office during pleasure; we order you for the next three years to recite once a-week the seven penitential psalms."

Had Galileo stood up boldly in defence of his opinions, he might not perhaps have disarmed the persecuting spirit

of the Inquisitors, but he might have confounded their ac-
cusations, and either stood the free champion of truth, or
fallen the proud martyr of science.   He had observation
and experience on his side against which no one could shut
his eyes; he had arguments to advance which could neither
be eluded nor contradicted; and more, he had the precedent
of the church itself acknowledging, and in a manner pat-
ronizing the very opinions for holding which they were persecuting him.   At the very moment that he stood clothed
in penitential sackcloth before the bar of the Inquistion, the
work of Corpernicus (himself a Catholic priest), dedicated
to the Pope, stood in the library of the Vatican ; and in the
very year of Galileo's first persecution, a work was issued
by a Carmelite monk at Naples, upholding the same opinions, and its author never called in question.   By confessing
to the charges of the Inquisition, Galileo in a manner jus-
tified its proceedings.   And, however detrimental it may
have been to the interests of science, however degrading to
the spirit of humanity, we must look upon the ancient philosopher with a kindly eye.   He lived in a time when the
mind of society was bound down in reverence and fear to
the dictates of the church.   His expanded mind might in
its vigor have braved persecution, and even death, before
perjuring himself in the eyes of the world.   But old age
had laid its withering hand upon him ; physical suffering
had broken down his frame; and, dreading to sigh out his
few remaining days in the lonely dungeons of the inquisition, he quailed before the dread power of that fearful in-
stitution, and passively renounced, in words, those opinions
which he knew to be true, and which the progress of science
has since demonstrated.   On his knees, and with his hand
upon the Scriptures, he solemnly abjured the opinions he had
taught, in the following words:

   "With a sincere heart and unfeigned faith, I abjure, curse, and detest
the said errors and heresies, (viz., that the earth moves, &c.)   I swear

that I will never in future say or assert anything, verbally, or in writing, which may give rise to a similar suspicion against me,

" I, Galileo Galilei, have abjured as above with my own hand."

Rising from his knees, Galileo, it is said, stamped with his foot upon the ground, and whispered to a friend, "*It does move, though.*"

Immediately on the ceremony being concluded, Galileo was conducted to the prisons of the Inquisition. The abjuration and sentence were publicly read in the principal universities. After four days' confinement, the interest of the Duke of Tuscany procured his liberty to reside under surveillance in the house of the Tuscan ambassador, from whence he was shortly removed to the palace of the archbishop Piccolomoni, at Sienna. Here he resided six months, and was kindly treated; he was then permitted to return to his own home, near Florence; still, however, under restraint. Shortly after returning home, Galileo suffered great affliction from the loss of his favorite daughter. From 1634 to 1638, he remained a prisoner in his own house, during nearly the whole of which time he suffered greatly from ill-health —every application for a remission of his sentence being rejected.

In 1638, he obtained leave to visit Florence, for the benefit of his health; but under such strict terms, that he dared neither visit his friends nor admit them to his house, and required even a special order to be allowed to attend mass. From 1633 to 1638, Galileo, who applied himself as closely to study as his health would permit, composed his " Dialogues on Local Motion." So fearful were his enemies that the true spirit of the philosopher might again break out, that a license was not granted for its publication, and it had to be printed in Holland.

About 1636, Galileo discovered the moon's diurnal and longitudinal libration. This was his last telescopic discovery. He had for years been afflicted with disease in the right eye; in 1637 his left was also attacked, and in a few months the bodily eyes of the philosopher were darkened forever. After publishing his Dialogues on Motion, he renewed his attempts to introduce his system of finding the longitude at sea. He made offers to the Dutch government, who appointed commissioners to investigate the subject. This correspondence ended in nothing. Galileo was presented with a golden chain as a token of respect; and after his blindness one of his pupils undertook to arrange and complete his calculations and observations. All parties engaged in this matter died before it could be brought before the world. This, however, is the less to be regretted; for the method proposed has never yet been found answerable to the desired purpose.

After Galileo had become blind, the Inquisition exercised a little more lenity towards their victim. Many eminent men of the day visited him, among whom was Milton. He projected a continuation of his Dialogues on Motion; but while preparing it, he was seized with his last illness, and in two months the spirit of the injured philosopher was removed from the enmity of his persecutors. Not content, however, with striking him down while living, the vengeance of the Inquisition followed Galileo even in death. His right to make a will, and of being buried in consecrated ground was disputed; and although these were withdrawn, his friends were prohibited from erecting a monument over his remains, and his body lay for thirty years buried in an obscure corner of the church. In 1737, his body was exhumed and re-interred under the splendid monument which now covers it. On this monument is a bust of Galileo, and figures of geometry and astronomy. His house at Arcetri, about a mile from Florence, still remains, an interesting relic to lovers of science.

——" Let the moon
Shine on thee in thy solitary walk ;
And let the misty mountain winds be free
To blow against thee ; and in after years,
When these wild ecstasies shall be matured
Into a sober pleasure—when thy mind
Shall be a mansion for all lovely forms,
Thy memory be a dwelling place
For all sweet sounds and harmonies, oh ! then
If solitude, or fear, or pain, or grief
Should be thy portion, with what healing thoughts
Of tender joy wilt thou remember me
And these my benedictions !"—WORDSWORTH.

Lightning Source UK Ltd.
Milton Keynes UK
UKHW022005080421
381687UK00003B/111